Failure Is An Option

An Attempted Memoir

H. Jon Benjamin

DUTTON

DUTTON

An imprint of Penguin Random House LLC
375 Hudson Street
New York, New York 10014

All book and insert illustrations by David Silver
Insert album covers © 2017 by Joel Gordon

LIBRARY OF CONGRESS CATALOGING-IN-PUBLICATION DATA

Names: Benjamin, H. Jon author.
Title: Failure is an option : an attempted memoir / H. Jon Benjamin.
Description: New York : Dutton, 2018.
Identifiers: LCCN 2017044297| ISBN 9781524742164 (hardback) |
ISBN 9781524742171 (ebook)
Subjects: LCSH: Benjamin, H. Jon. | Actors—United States—Biography. |
Conduct of life—Humor. | BISAC: HUMOR / Form / Essays. | BIOGRAPHY
& AUTOBIOGRAPHY / Entertainment & Performing Arts. | PERFORMING
ARTS / Comedy.
Classification: LCC PN2287.B4275 A3 2018 | DDC 791.4302/8092 [B]—dc23
LC record available at https://lccn.loc.gov/2017044297

Printed in the United States of America
1 3 5 7 9 10 8 6 4 2

BOOK DESIGN BY CASSANDRA GARRUZZO

While the author has made every effort to provide accurate telephone numbers, Internet addresses, and other contact information at the time of publication, neither the publisher nor the author assumes any responsibility for errors or for changes that occur after publication. Further, the publisher does not have any control over and does not assume any responsibility for author or third-party websites or their content.

Penguin is committed to publishing works of quality and integrity. In that spirit, we are proud to offer this book to our readers; however, the story, the experiences, and the words are the author's alone.

*For all of you failures out there. You CAN do worse.
Also, for Amy, Judah, Howard, Shirley, and Jodi. I know I
have failed you, but I wrote a book?*

Contents

CONTENTS

Acknowledgments

Before we go any further, I have some things I need to acknowledge.

I have let myself go. No doubts about it. I have been trying, but the pulling of time has rendered me soft and flatulent, like so much sour taffy.

I smell. Aging organic form starts to take on malodor, like fermentation. I cover it with a variety of applied scents, but I still am starting to smell of what I imagine the seventeenth century smelled like. Like rotting food and manure with an occasional whiff of sulfur. If I pass by, light a match.

Also, this book could have been better if any number of other writers, many who I know personally, would have written it.

Some of the material in this book is most likely pilfered from other writers. Most likely Leopold Allen, a writing partner of mine who hopefully won't sue.

I am writing this at the dawn of the Trump presidency,

particularly apropos of failure being an option. A very horrible and dangerous option in the case of an entire country's future.

I did initially want to call this book *Hide This Book* and print only one copy and then hide it. And then, if somebody found it, they would need to hide it again. And so forth.

Prologue
(the Preliminary Failure
Before the Main Failure)

Everything I didn't do has gotten me
to where I am.

—H. Jon Benjamin

A ll right! Here we go! My third sentence of my first book and I'm already really tired of writing, but I promise you, this will be worth it. And let's face it—you probably paid very little for this. Based on how much you paid, this book might be one of the best bargains you have ever pulled off in your life *and* with no real negotiation. That's what I did for you. I let the market decide, and that empowers you. A classic objectivist proposition. It is what makes America great again and again and again. And that isn't just a cheap saying peddled by some psychotic charlatan with weird hair (but having said all that, it may be a good campaign slogan for Donald Trump Jr.—"Make America great again, AGAIN." Thank me later, Donny Jr.), but, in my case a real promise.

When I was saddled with the task of writing a book, I had to dig shallow to think about what it is I had to say to you, my gentle reader . . . and also you, my rough reader. Not enough attention has been given to all you rough readers out there. But I can assure you, I'm no Charlotte Brontë or Miss Manners. I'm gonna go for it, without any real sense of literary consequence. A true path paver. A pioneer, armed with a keyboard and a keen eye for "taking it to the limit." Many will be confounded by what they read, many or all will be disappointed, but all of you will be part of this most exhilarating experiment in textual synergy. You and I together forever, locked in eternal struggle—writer and reader forever entwined. A twisted commingling of semiconsensual, transmodal logical consequence. I write, you read. A self-contained system, like a less scatological human caterpillar (I say *less*, because you may read this on the toilet).

On that note, let me guide you, and I will try and take you to the end of the rainbow. A place that is cold but cordial. A place that is waiting for you, with faceless determination. The end. That is what we are here for—the end. Together till the end.

What I am doing right now is single-handedly providing you with the means to a literal end. And I will give it, like a lightning bolt. And you will rejoice! And then you will rest in the afterglow all flushed and enervated, realizing that I fulfilled my promise to you: to end this book.

(In French) Oh, darkness I wait for your embrace
The death before death
words choke my breath
But the end is sweet relief
Jon Benjamin's book
(Sorry, couldn't afford a French translator)

Anyway, what is this book? Well, in the simplest terms, all I have is my story. But looking at it with a critical eye, my story is something of a cautionary tale. It is the story of a failure. But by the same token, it is an aspirational tale, in that most failures never get to tell their tales. Who would listen? You know the old saying "History is written by the victors." It's like that. Failures are a voiceless mass of unrealized promise. Where would we be if this world was solely composed of failures? By nature, survival itself is a narrative imbued with a success imperative. I mean, science itself compels that argument. It's survival of the fittest, not survival of the fattest. But that would be a good name for a game show: *Survival of the Fattest.* By no means, though, am I connecting fat with fail, it just happened to work as an alliterative.

To be clear, this is a polemic in favor of failure. It's an assertion that failure is an option and even, at times, a viable prescription for a better life, despite its long-standing stigmatization. Failure can be incredibly freeing and an end in itself, not just that tired platitude that it is a necessary step on the road to success. Despite my own success, I maintain that failure is my prevailing life force and my success has been a parallel and unrelated condition, not a consequence of my failure(s). If you're not following, that's because I'm a failure. Or because you're a failure. But either way, that's a good thing.

Hopefully, this book will serve to give people prone to seek success more reason to pull back, and for those who already are failing, a reason to continue to do so with a sense of purpose. That said, unbridled failure can be a pretty overwhelming thing, and people do need mechanisms in place to use their will to fail reasonably and in good taste. There are limits, even with failure, and I don't want to set any of you on a path toward sitting in a dark room with cardboard covering your windows and feces (yours) smeared on the walls and the floor—unless it is a clever version of a surprise party. The task at hand is to bring failure into your life, accept it, and then find the right amount that suits you. A failure balance, or an FB, if you will.

I can't claim this is the manual of failure, but maybe this is the story or stories that some future civilization will look at and use as the example of how civilization started to embrace failure—like a new bible for the inevitable dystopian future. If you think of this book in those terms, we are really onto something special here. Let me give you a quick example and then I'll get to how I personally failed and how I represent all of us. It is a classic story of failure and it comes from the Bible, but my interpretation is more useful (sorry, Athanasius Kircher). It is the story of Noah and the Flood.

As the story goes, humankind had become self-absorbed and wicked and turned their backs on the word of God, except for Noah and his family, who remained annoyingly righteous. God chose Noah as his emissary, to tell the people to repent or face the wrath of God. The people laughed *hard* at Noah (because they were wicked and most probably drunk) and his do-goody attitude. God then told Noah that, because the people failed to heed his warning, he would bring upon them a flood that would destroy humanity, only sparing Noah, his family, and a collection of animals. Noah sent the message, to which the people laughed *hard* in his face. And you know the outcome—God instructed the building of the ark, and Noah and his family were spared, to carry forward human civilization.

Here's the basic problem. As Noah failed to convince the people to bow to the will of God, God failed us by choosing Noah to get the word out. And here we are today, the product of a failed guy and, to a greater degree, a failed God, who trusted the wrong person to do his bidding and then punished humanity for his own faulty methodology. Basically, God was way too needy. This kind of attitude is all over the Bible: God always being mad at his creations and doling out disproportional punishment. It's certainly not a fair fight, pitting humans against omnipotence.

So here's my assessment based on little to no research: basically "just wingin' it" (great name for an airline, by the way) but in a thoughtful way. Humanity is now made up of primarily people driven by a complete repudiation of failure and, ipso facto, are compelled psychologically and sociologically to succeed. But because only a tiny majority can fulfill this due to the simple fact that more than 98 percent of the population are not qualified to achieve real success, we need to come to a general understanding that failure is good for society.

Let's take any simple job as an example: carpenter (since Noah was mentioned). It is my contention that more than 98 percent of carpenters are subpar at their craft. There are approximately one million carpenters in the United States, according to the Bureau of Labor Statistics, so, based on my theory, there are only about twenty thousand decent carpenters. The rest, whether they know it or not, are bad but are likely pretending to be good (just wingin' it). This theory can be applied to everyone: doctors, lawyers, bankers, cooks, therapists, personal trainers . . .

Widespread self-knowledge and acceptance of one's own biological inadequacies would set off a chain reaction that would help the successful be more successful and relieve those who outreach their given capacities, creating a huge uptick in happiness. In simple terms, be less driven.

Soon enough, the path to failure would become a viable option. If a person doesn't feel the need to succeed, then they won't try so hard, creating a quasi utopia. And this would move our success-oriented culture toward a more natural lazy state for humankind. It's like that old syrupy proverb "Teach a man to fish . . ." In my version, it would be "Give a man a fish, and he'll eat for a day;

teach a man to fish, and he'll eat for a lifetime, *but* he'll probably come to really hate fishing, so just give him a fish *and* teach him to fish."

With that, I will now regale you with some personal stories of failure in my life. I have failed in so many ways; it's hard to tell all the stories. Failure is enmeshed in my DNA. For every single action taken, there are multiple, sometimes thousands of micro failures. And what might appear inconsequential to the naked eye, like a brief stammer or a quick sniffle, in my mind is a cascading and ever-expanding sandstorm of self-doubt and self-recrimination. Talk to me for even a minute and you'll think, "Wow, nice guy," but in my mind, the cobwebs of failure are spinning and proliferating like a cotton candy machine.

It may be too late for little old me, but you, YOU! You can fail and be happy.

CHAPTER 1

The Early Failure Years (or How I Failed to Have a Name)

I was born in a hospital. I was told that my mother was given nitrous oxide for the birth. As in, she was totally sedated. The whole labor, totally out of it. My father used to say it was used for the conception as well. Just kidding, he never said that. I just wanted to make a salty joke and blame it on my father. Anyway, they used strange methods back in the sixties. Maybe her sedation affected me. I do feel dizzy all the time, and I'm incredibly lazy, which might have all been connected to not having heard the agonized screams of my mother as I came into the world. Just entering the universe to a really quiet room, but for the nasal mutterings of a Jewish obstetrician complaining to a nurse about the cost of his landscaper, can have a lasting effect on one's personality.

The place of my birth was Worcester, Massachusetts. Worcester isn't known for its good hospitals, so I imagine

I was mishandled. I don't have any visible signs of that, except for two huge indentions in my skull. I assume forceps were used. I read once that the name Elliot became popular in the late nineteenth century because that was the name of the forceps used in childbirth: the Elliot forceps. Can you imagine naming your child after the steel instrument that pulled them out of your vagina? That shows a real lack of due diligence. When you name your child after a medical device, it is a pretty telltale sign of an unhappy marriage. Not many women naming their kids Eppy today, after the epidural. Just saying. Also, that will be the last time I will write "just saying," based on how I cringed after writing it.

I was named Harry Jon Benjamin. Harry after my paternal grandfather and Jon after the misspelling of John. It appears that there was some discord over my name, so an untidy agreement was made between my parents where they would maintain my first name on the birth certificate but call me by my middle name.

The Harry has always been a buried secret, like an identity Easter egg, and that mystery has had its own odd effects as well, probably due to the fact that my dad's father died at a really young age, so passing on his name would be like passing on a curse. But they still gave it anyway, with the caveat of deciding to never utter it. So, as a result, I am just subtly cursed by the ghosts of my ancestry. It's a very Jewish tendency to honor and excise the past simultaneously. (Jewish voice) "He's named after his grandfather, God rest his soul, a name that will never

ever be uttered in this house, God forbid!" That's what's in my name. A real Jewish cocktail of guilt, pride, and necrophobia.

Still, Jon is a pretty solid mainstream name, so I could blend in, until teachers read out the spelling. It's never fun to get made fun of for the fact your name is spelled wrong. Like, "Your mom's so dumb, she spelled John wrong." Or "How dare you sully the memory of John the Baptist, who baptized Jesus and whose head was cut clean off by King Herod just 'cause his vindictive daughter asked him to!" Anyway, no one is ever completely scarred by a name, except for, maybe, that guy named Tiny Ichicock.

My earliest memories are of my parents cleaning. My father owned an electrical supply store that sold lighting and bulbs and circuit breakers, etc., so as a family, we had access to a lot of cutting-edge electrical equipment. You know how in the fifties, there was a rush to be the first home on the block to purchase a TV set? It was momentous, a real sea change for families. That "moment" came for us in the form of the NuTone Central Vacuum System. Because of my father's position, we were definitely the first home in our neighborhood to install the vac system, which held the promise of changing everything for home cleaning. It was basically a network of ports in the wall of any room that could connect a vacuum hose to a central unit in the basement. A comprehensive cleaning system, like the *2001: A Space Odyssey* of vacuum systems. A real Valhalla for compulsive cleaners.

And shit, did they use it. In my memory, most of my

childhood was spent vacuuming or hearing the sound of vacuuming. Giving my parents this technology was like giving the Union forces the Gatling gun—you can do so much more damage so much more quickly. And with more frequency. The key element to the NuTone vac was that you could increase the sheer amount of "cleaning" opportunities in any given moment. As in, it encouraged rapid-response cleaning. Like, if one piece of lint was on the floor, one could, or dare I say, *should*, plug in the vac and deal with it like it was a medical emergency.

With the vacuum in place, our house was on its way to becoming "clear." As in, a perfectly self-contained cleaning environment. A real biosphere of neuroses. The plaintive wails of the NuTone vac system would wake me in the morning and put me to sleep at night. A giant sucking sound, if you will. And I never knew when and where it was going to come. The threat was always nigh. I would lie awake in bed and long for the simpler times, when vacuums were manual.

From the eyes of this child, this was just the way things were. Futuristic cleaning all the time and without any foreseeable slackening. The sheer force of constant cleaning was, of course, the veneer of order for a bubbling chaos beneath, and new technologies would only serve to stiffen that veneer. To this day, I can't clean. And that seems counterintuitive to the bulk of my upbringing, which was consumed with it. Maybe it was rebellion, or maybe I'm still in a state of shock, but to this day, I wipe off a table as if you handed a baby monkey a wet cloth.

I still get bizarre pleasure in watching people clean, though. One of the first things I did after making some money was hire a cleaning woman to come to my studio apartment in New York City. She was young and cute, but it was less sexual attraction than an attraction to the cleaning. I would sit and marvel at it, which made for an uncomfortable situation. There was always this very present energy coming from her, saying, "Why are you always hanging around here in your small apartment and watching me clean?" My intentions were very easy to misread, and it was a hard distinction to communicate, like, "I'm not gawking at you the way you're thinking. I just like to watch people clean. Because of my childhood. Seriously I just need to watch!"

CHAPTER 2

How I Failed at Pretty Much Everything as a Kid (the Foundations of Failure)

I meet kids all the time lately who are really good at things, and I keep thinking, I don't remember being good at anything as a kid. My son, who is fourteen now, has many talented friends, some who play music, others who are savvy at coding; others speak several languages, some are precocious artists, etc. Mainly, as a kid, I just went to Friendly's. And I had so much time to get good at something, but no . . . nothing. A local pederast did try to get me into archery, but I even faltered at that, which I guess was a good thing: the avoiding pederasty part.

But why was I so averse to getting good at something? I remember this one kid in my elementary school who was an avid Cub Scout. He recruited me to join his Cub troop that was run by his father. His skill was that he knew how to tie something like five hundred different knots. So many knots. The double loop, the half hitch, the midline loop, the sailor's hitch, the strangle knot, even the super controversial hangman's knot. I went to one scout meeting at his house and we sat in a tent for at least two hours tying knots using a diagrammatic guide. He looked so happy. After the meeting, I immediately quit the Cub Scouts.

I often wonder if that kid finally ever hung himself or others. More likely, he's just an incredibly successful scout leader. But he was doing something, despite its being only tying knots. He was practicing sophisticated skills, even at nine years old. I recall reading about Ben Franklin, who left school at ten, apprenticed with his brother as a printer, then started writing for a newspaper at age fifteen. Jesus. I mean, c'mon. What a prodigious asshole.

My unique talents centered more around watching TV while eating SpaghettiOs raw from the can, which made my father rabidly mad, because he had installed in the TV room a white shag rug, that, as a consequence, had recurring and ever-growing concentric SpaghettiO stains. Also, I was proficient at taking a racquetball racket and hitting a tennis ball in my living room against the wide brick chimney for hours. That's a skill I could have possibly developed into something greater, but on the whole, it was more like what one would do for recreation in a supermax. And don't get me wrong: everyone's childhood is "like a prison," even though that's a bit "reductio ad custodia." But, look, starting early being "into some-

thing" has its consequences, too. One can carry that burden, heavy, of having tied all those knots.

For me, I just needed to find my own thing. Anything
that would envelop my time beyond procrastination.
Something that would set me on a higher path. The thing
is, I was very shy and introverted. I didn't realize that
then, but I enjoyed being home alone, despite the accom-
panying gripping loneliness. One thing I started to do
was record myself on a Panasonic cassette player doing
interviews. But because I seldom left my house, I would
interview me as me or me as other people.

This turned out to be a relatively successful pet project,
most evident in the time I interviewed myself as an astronaut on *Voyager 1* and played it for all the kids at school
and they went crazy. It, in a nutshell, exemplified the
power of lying.

My hoax was so convincing that one student coaxed
me to play it for our teachers. I played it for Mr. Simko,
our gym teacher, and he was shocked. He asked me how
I got to interview a real astronaut, and I told him that he
came to my house because he was friendly with our neighbor who was a scientist.

Then I played it for my homeroom teacher Mr. Pow-
ers, and he immediately pointed out that *Voyager 1* was
unmanned.

"Oh . . . yeah, but he was in the space program."

"But he described seeing Earth from the spacecraft on
Voyager One."

"Well, he must have been joking."

"But the whole interview was about him being in space."

"He must have been talking about a different spaceship."

"And as far I know, Jon, there is no astronaut in NASA named Biff Alderman."

I really should have stopped with the gym teacher, but that's the price one pays when one flies too close to the sun, or, in other words, plays a fake interview with an astronaut for a guy who has a completist knowledge of the space program.

Later, I tried school politics. In sixth grade, I ran for class treasurer. My only real experience with money thus far had been borrowing it from my parents and stealing it from my cousin's drawer. Both seemed ample qualifiers to run for treasurer. My decision to run was somewhat quixotic, as in I decided to run the day of the elections.

I was up against a girl named Doreen. She was smart, driven, and self-assured. She was running unopposed and had made signs to "Vote Doreen" and hung them all over the school. I was what is now called a "spoiler candidate." In the auditorium, in front of the class, Doreen gave her speech. It was well delivered and she spoke eloquently about raising funds to support a class trip to Boston. That was huge.

Though we were only an hour from Boston, it was like a galaxy away for most people in Worcester. Personally, I had been only a few times, but most kids talked about Boston like it was Paris. Like, "Have you been to Boston?" "Are you fucking kidding me? No fucking way. I've been to Shrewsbury, though."

She talked about working with the teachers and the school board to raise money for this trip to go to Paul Revere's house. She also talked about getting new outdoor equipment for the playground. New balls, new baseball equipment, and new nets for the basketball hoops.

I thought I had this in the bag. I was counting on the "no-nothing" vote. Nobody wants some loudmouth, proactive girl with a solid agenda, making promises about school trips and better overall conditions. Give them something they really want to hear: a hopeless message, a message that conveys "you get what you get." Why invest in new balls when we've been kicking around that one deflated one for *years*? Do we really want to sully the memory of all those who came before us who kicked that deflated ball? Do we want some shiny new netting on the hoop when our forefathers played without them? What we needed was some hard-line illiberalism.

Instead, she completed her speech, and I was called up and I stood before the class, immediately drowning in flop sweat, and said, "What she said."

Everybody stared and the room started to melt and no one even uttered a chuckle. Even the heater hissed in disapproval. I received zero votes. Later that year, I looked over at Doreen while we stood in Paul Revere's dumb bedroom and she gave me a smug look. Whatever.

I tried music. My father played the clarinet. But he had stopped playing by the time I was born, so it was more my dad had a clarinet. My dad also had a gun. He never shot it. I guess it was for protection. He kept it hidden in a box somewhere on a shelf in the back of a hallway closet—a perfect spot for a gun when you need one quickly. In the event of a home invasion, my father would have to exchange pleasantries with the intruders, all the while subtly making his way to a closet at the other side of the house to get the gun. Or maybe his plan all along was to deceive them by telling them that he keeps all his money in a wooden box in a hall closet, then lure them to this closet and then, after using a stepladder to reach up to the shelf for the box, slowly open it, pull out the pistol, and say, "Oh, my mistake, this was the box with *this* in it," then BLAM BLAM BLAM, shower them with bullets.

In any event, the gun and the clarinet basically served the same purpose, at least in my eyes. Just totems of some past life my dad lived that were now nothing more than relics, stuffed in a box, never to be seen or used. That was a pretty awesome imagined past life, though, filled with guns and clarinets. Maybe he was in the illegal woodwind mafia.

Anyway, he was, in reality, a jazz fan—mainly, from his album collection, "white jazz," as in big band—Benny Goodman, Glenn Miller, Tommy Dorsey, etc. (Although, to be fair, there were black musicians in big bands.) He did tell stories of traveling to New York City when he was younger and going to jazz clubs, but the only black artist I remember him listening to was Paul Robeson. There's nothing better after a quiet dinner with family, heading into the living room and putting on some intensely solemn spirituals to get the mood up. That's how my family rolled . . . da old chariot along. (That's a solid Paul Robeson joke, if you like those.)

Even as a younger kid, I never took to learning an instrument. I took lessons on the recorder (the world's worst instrument, with the exception of the steam calliope) for several years, then switched to the violin, whereupon I failed miserably at the Suzuki method—a cruel, psyopsstyle method of forcing children to make music, and after that, finally landed on the guitar. To my chagrin, I had and have painfully short fingers, so even with a children's guitar, it was hard to play a chord, but thankfully that didn't matter to my guitar teacher, who would come to my house with his girlfriend, sit me down in front of our stereo, put on an album, and have me strum to it, while he and his girlfriend left the room. I assumed this was how lessons worked, and only later realized he should pay my parents back for both the lessons and for the use of my sister's room to have sex in.

After that, it was all downhill with my becoming musical in any way. I could play the drums a bit. In fact, I "played" the drums at our school's sixth-grade talent show, because the drummer of the band didn't show and they asked me to fill in. I told them that I had never played on a drum set before, and the lead singer said, just sit there and hold up the sticks and wave them around. So I sat there anxiously holding my sticks in the air, occasion-ally moving them like a navy signalman, while the band played "Smoke on the Water."

After, I asked, "Why did you even bother having me?" He told me, "We set up the drum set, so . . ." Many kids came up to me after and said, "Great job." Only Alan Leiter asked, "Why didn't you play?" I plainly stated, "I can't," and he shrugged and said, "Oh, cool." Maybe this was the template that set me on the road to relishing the role of "proudly unaccomplished."

So, higher path. How do you get on one? One can employ what I call the torpor technique. It's essentially this: when you discover you're not good at anything, wait. Wait until you know something changes, and you will feel that change when it happens. You will inevitably get a lot of resistance from those who will try to get you to be good at something, but don't let this deter you from waiting. I waited. I mean, it took until two years ago till I made an album based on *not* being able to play piano (titled *Well, I Should Have . . . Learned How to Play Piano*), and if, per-chance, I had learned as a kid, I would not have been able to do that. I waited forty years, and something came of it.

And, I will say, the album turned out to be a rather productive experiment of creative fission, or friction, to bring together in one moment, those who can and one who can't and both make something together. It was a pure example of democracy at work. A professional jazz trio, with me on piano. Recorded for posterity. And it resonated.

Just recently, I went to my local health food market to buy some avocados, and as I was checking out, the woman behind the register looked up slowly and grimaced ever so slightly and then timidly said, "Can I ask you a question?"

I said sure.

Then she said, with a bitterness in her voice, "Why would you make that jazz album if you can't play jazz?"

"Why wouldn't I?" I said.

She sneered.

See how failure works out sometimes? Even for a kid who couldn't get good at anything.

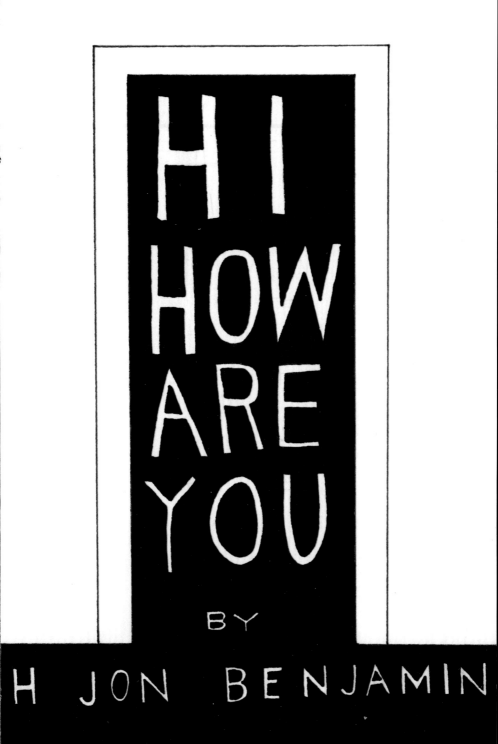

Hi, how are you?

I hope you are
doing well.

I know we've
never met.

But does my
face ring a
bell?

I only came to tuck you in and kiss you on the cheek . . . and to tell you everything's all right and have a good night's sleep.

Well, I best
be going;
I've got a
lot to do.

If you ever
need to talk
to me . . .

Just have
your mom
open this
book and
read it again
to you.

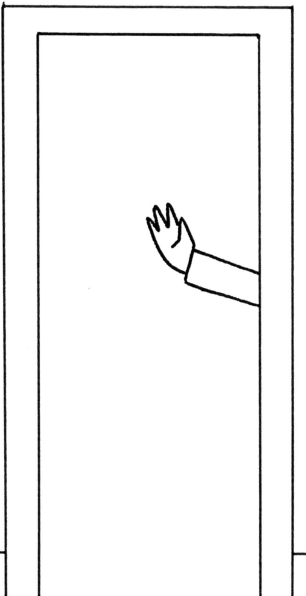

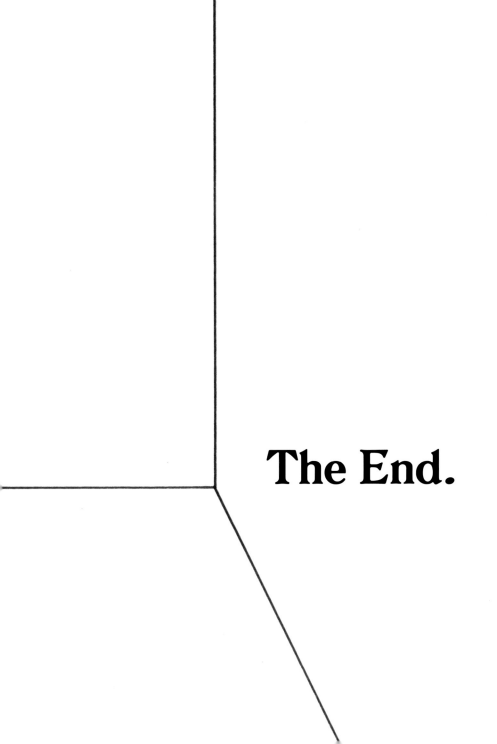

The End.

Failed Bands I've Been In

CHAPTER 3

The Sleepover
(and How I Failed to Have One)

The first kid I remember wanting to switch lives with was my friend James. He was my friend in elementary school. My school was a depressing municipal brick building filled with tough white kids and unhappy teachers. There were no young teachers. They all seemed like relics. Angry, ossified men and women plodding on till retirement. I remember only one teacher who seemed positive and inspired learning, but he had chronic stomach pain, like a perpetual ulcer, so while drinking liquid antacid, most of his class involved him doubled over in anguish. But in the scant moments when he actually taught, he was worthy.

My friend James had this huge smile. He was always smiling. He seemed happy. I think he was the happiest kid I knew. I assume that's why I wanted to be him. James and I hung out a lot. James and I shared many firsts. The first candy I stole was with James. The first cigarette I tried to smoke was with James. The first erection I saw was with James. No, it wasn't his. Or mine. Or the teacher who had ulcers. Let me elaborate.

Our route walking home took us down a main street. The street had no parking, but once, walking home, we saw a car parked on the side of the road. James ran ahead and looked in the passenger window. I was quick to follow. In the driver's seat, a man sat vigorously masturbating. It felt like we watched for a good thirty seconds. Two little kids with their heads in a car window watching an obscene act like a puppet show. He didn't stop. He just looked at us, signaling with his eyes down as if to say to us, "Check this out." We did. And then we ran away quickly.

I will always remember that guy. If he's reading this right now . . . Hey. Although I imagine he's probably passed away. And on his gravestone, it reads: HERE LIES (INSERT NAME), PUBLIC MASTURBATOR.

The other first with James was a sleepover. James invited me to his house. I had actually never before been to his house. Suffice it to say, I was uneasy about it. My parents were comforting and suggested I take my blanket, whose name was Blanky. That helped. Having Blanky always helped.

Let me quickly digress. I have always been interested in becoming someone else. I think it's a common trait. Dysphoria may be the psychological term for it. Or psychosis. When I was really young, I would wander into dysphoric states all the time. Mainly this involved going up to other people, standing near them, and trying to imagine what it would be like if I were them.

The danger, of course, was of it actually happening. I thought about this a lot. It was like early onset existential dread. Maybe it was because I was essentially an only child (my sister was six years older) and both my parents worked and left me alone a lot. I was pretty much a latchkey kid. My after-school regimen was pouring State Line potato chips into a mixing bowl and then pouring vinegar over them, making a mash, then eating it with a spoon like soup. Potato chip soup. Then, sitting and watching TV with the aforementioned potato chip soup, intermittently hitting a tennis ball against a wall. Sad, but very helpful in developing hand-eye coordination and high blood pressure simultaneously.

My family used to go on summer vacations to the beach in Ogunquit, Maine, and this beach was always crammed with people. At high tide, people were penned in between the ocean and the dunes on a narrow strip of beach that spanned a good distance, maybe a mile. A sea of people—families, kids, teenagers, boyfriends and girlfriends, old and young, black (well not really—it's Maine) and white. So mostly white.

Gay and straight for sure, though. Ogunquit had an out gay-tourist community. There were tons of Canadian gays. Canadian gays are some of the best gays in the world. So clean. So healthy. So full of hope. So fulsome in their Speedos. They're not just gay, they're g-eh. That could be a T-shirt. Seriously.

Ogunquit Beach was ripe for a boy with dysphoria. I could roam around and get lost in so many other people's worlds. I recall one family let me stand right next to them and watch them for what seemed like hours. After some time, I think they forgot I was there. It was more than eavesdropping. And more than voyeurism. It was a kind of visual transubstantiation. If I watched them, I became them.

Back to the sleepover. James's house was a typical Worcester house, a modest antique wood-shingled house among similarly styled homes, tightly packed onto a side street. My memory of the interior is a little foggy, but I remember that the living room and dining room were connected and there was a couch and a recliner, and if memory serves, many crosses on the wall, like Carrie's house. James had a brother who was older, maybe fourteen, and he was home upstairs with his friends. I don't remember the mom even being there, but she must have been. Or maybe not. Like I said before, things were pretty loosey-goosey back in the seventies.

I think we read magazines and drank soda, then his dad came home. And that's when things went south really fast. Remember, first sleepover, very nervous, lots of crosses on the wall, and then . . . let me digress again.

My parents were pretty quiet people. There was a lot of quiet talking. Or no talking, but if we talked it was at a reasonably low volume. Like one would imagine people talking in East Berlin before the wall came down: everything in hushed tones, to avoid the Stasi listening in. The only thing missing was someone putting on an LP really loud, like big band music, to further mute the conversation.

I don't recall my parents ever fighting. Overall, it was a home dictated by an unspoken order of cautious and orderly behavior. There was a cloak of courtly servility, like if Louis XVI and Marie Antoinette lived modestly in central Massachusetts surrounded by microwaved tuna casserole. If they did have a fight, my dad would quietly leave and then come home a few hours later. But because it was so unclear as to whether they had a fight, he might have been just going out. Very, very difficult to discern.

In any case, that lifestyle did not prepare me for James's dad. I didn't know it, but I think he was very drunk. Or just having a bad day because someone pushed him into a whiskey barrel. He was very angry at James. Also, very angry at James's brother. It was an immediate hailstorm of anger. He sat in the recliner and yelled for a long time. I can't remember what about, but it was loud and it was emotive and I was stunned. I had never seen anything like this. I loved it.

I now see what I didn't then, but all I could see then was this crazy emotive chaos. So new and different. James's mood soured fast. And I just stood there watching this horrible spectacle, completely rapt. Eventually, James took me aside and told me we were going to sleep outside to get away. *W-w-what?* Allegedly, there was a tent in the backyard that he set up for when his dad was acting the way he was. The tent was essentially fifteen feet from the house, and the backyard was small, with a fence around it. So I brought Blanky and we went to the tent.

Camping out wasn't a familiar occurrence in my life. I had certainly never done it. My parents once signed me up for a one-week trip to 4-H camp, which was going to involve a one-night campout, which I dreaded, but that never happened because on the first night at the camp, a girl attempted suicide, fortunately canceling the camp altogether.

As grim as James's family situation looked to me— singularly the most poignantly tragic picture of a broken family I could conceive of, replete with a dad so mean the son actually set up a tent on his property to escape him— my focus was still more on how not to sleep outside, now that we were officially outside.

A few minutes later, James and I were in the tent, and it was kind of cold, and he had a flashlight, and I really didn't know how to talk to a kid who was clearly having a total shit life. I felt bad, but I was also cold and brimming with anxiety. I couldn't really go inside, though, because I was with James, and his apparently drunk, angry dad was in there, so I was stuck in this bizarre limbo.

I waited. He finally fell asleep, and it must have been at least midnight, and I was lying faceup in mortal terror. Frozen and frozen. I was also afraid to go outside the tent, because those fifteen feet between tent and house were, in my estimation, a vast chasm of untold horror.

Finally, with everything I could gather, I got up and sprinted inside and felt my way around the kitchen like Clarice in the final sequence of *Silence of the Lambs* till I found the phone and quietly called my parents. I snuck out the front door and stood in the street until my dad came around. I jumped in his car, leaving without waking James in his tent.

The first sleepover was a clear failure, but in retrospect, the best one I've ever had. I mean, there were no bedtime games, homemade cookies, or building a fort, just tension, a family in crisis, and sitting in a cold tent for three hours. That was more my scene. I'm not even sure whether James ever asked me why I wasn't there in the morning. He just smiled and moved on. Maybe that's why I wanted to be him.

CHAPTER 4

The Robbery
(and How I Failed to Stop One)

My neighborhood growing up was quiet—
mundane, even. People kept to themselves.
It wasn't unfriendly, just staid. I didn't
really know most of my neighbors. I heard
one neighbor was agoraphobic and another was a judge
who allegedly had a gun. Just random bits of information,
maybe true, maybe not, about the people on my street.

In my early life there, two things stood out as unusual.
Once, my mother and I came home from shopping and
there was a horse in our yard. There were no horse farms
anywhere near where we lived, so a horse in our yard was
odd, maybe an omen, maybe a ghost horse. After seeing
us, it galloped away down our street and out of our lives
forever.

The other was one night, late, say around eleven, a car
kept driving up and down our street, with a girl screaming

in it. After some time, the neighbors slowly emerged from their homes trying to figure out what was going on. My mom was beside herself. She thought we were under siege. She doesn't do well in crisis situations, and although this wasn't a clear-cut crisis, I think just the hint of something awry put her in a state of abject terror.

The car went away, but a neighbor had passed along a tidbit of information that at the end of the street, in the woods, was a Styrofoam box of dry ice. The police arrived, but there was no explanation—just a girl in a car scream-ing and a random box of dry ice. It had the trappings of some satanic ritual but was more likely high school kids who stole from their science lab on a joy ride. But the pos-sibility of some satanic ritual in our little neighborhood was definitely alluring. Nice to have a little satanic shake-up once in a while in a sleepy New England town.

Our house was a third of the way up a side street lined with modest homes. The homes weren't on top of one an-other. Each enjoyed a little bit of land, so they were some-what spread out. Our house was a small A-frame with an orange door with a knob in the middle. A hint of eccen-tricity. Or was it a satanic symbol?

My parents had the house built so it was more modern than the other rather traditional ranch homes in the neighborhood. It had a wraparound deck from the front to the side. After school I would climb up on the deck to pretend like I was robbing the place. It was also easy to hoist myself onto the roof, which was another lonely hobby of mine: walking on a roof. Otherwise, I spent a lot of time bouncing a tennis ball against the front stairs or practicing archery. My dad bought a bale of hay and put it out back and hung a target that I could shoot at with my bow.

Mainly, I would have to occupy myself for the few hours before my parents would return from work doing any one or all of these things. Our house was on a slope that ran down to a fence, separating our property from the neighbors', and before the fence there were two giant willow trees, whose branches shielded the view from the neighbors below.

One afternoon, I decided it would be fun to play catch. But, seeing that I had nobody to do that with, I took my glove and ball and ventured out to play "tragicatch," a game I had invented that involved my throwing a ball up in the air, then catching it as it dropped. Really uncomplicated, like an outdoorsy, sportier version of solitaire.

Anyway, as I was in the middle of my game, I could hear my neighbor playing catch with his dad. My neighbors were a family of five—one kid was a little younger than me and two a bit older, say around thirteen or so. The mother had remarried and her new husband cut a rather handsome figure. He was tall and broad-shouldered, with an athletic build and a welcoming smile. He looked like a professional baseball player, or an ex-model or an ex–pro baseball player/model. On the surface, he was the dad any kid would want. Shit, he was even playing catch with his stepson and I was playing "tragicatch."

And, look, I liked my dad, it's just that this guy seemed

pretty perfect. My dad liked tennis and racquetball. Not that that's bad, but when you're a kid and someone asks you what your favorite sport is and you say racquetball, they likely pull down your pants and punch you in the dick. I really like baseball. I collected baseball cards. I played in Little League. My neighbor's dad seemed very into baseball. The thing was, I didn't really know them that well, and I wasn't the type to walk down and introduce myself.

So I hatched a plan to throw my baseball down into their yard, and when I ran down to retrieve it, I would pretend that my dad had thrown it. I rallied the courage and whipped the ball down and ran into their yard, yelling, "Jesus, Dad, terrible throw." I stumbled through the awkward lie about how I was playing up in my yard with my dad, too. Just another kid playing catch with his dad. Yeah, playing catch with the old man.

I'm fairly sure they knew I was lying, so after a few more bumbling attempts at conversation, they invited me to play. Right away, the dad began to teach me how to throw a curveball. I was in love. I'm a huge curveball fan. The curveball is the oral sex of baseball. It's delicate and precarious. Maybe a bad analogy, but maybe not. They never asked why my imaginary dad never came down, considering I purportedly left him there in the middle of a catch, over an hour and a half earlier.

Anyway, it was the beginning of a wonderful friendship. I quickly became close with them and they treated me like family. I soon got in the habit of going to their house after school instead of mine, because they would leave their sliding door in the back of the house open so I just could go in and wait for the kids to come home.

Also, as I recall, they had milk, and for some reason our house never had milk. Milk was really good. But I repeat, our house never had milk. I think it was a hold-over from the Jewish kosher laws (called kashruth), which dictate a separation of dairy and meat. This derived from a passage in the Bible, which states that no goat should be cooked in its own mother's milk.

Now, you could take this literally, because milk-soaked goat made the goat taste better, but it could be perceived (from the perspective of the human) as unusually cruel to the goat itself, its being cooked in its own mother's milk. Or, perhaps, if one could assign advanced goat cognition, then maybe it is aware enough to realize that it is being cooked in the very sustaining liquid from its loving mama. *Or* the Bible might have just been having a bit of fun with words, as in, figuratively, don't cook a goat in its own mother's milk, as in "don't be an asshole." Either way, this rule stuck, and even in the modern world, conservative Jewish homes sometimes have two kitchens, to enforce the law, separating the preparing and consuming of dairy products and meat products.

I'm not saying it was just the milk that attracted me to the neighbors, but that was a big part of it. They were decidedly not Jewish, and that had its allure. They were messy. Not overly messy, just not afraid to let things go. They had a dog. That was fun. The closest thing we had in our house to pets were plants.

Actually, once, for a very short time, we had a cat, but it was banished to the basement because it tracked dirt and ate from the floor. That soured our (the cat and my family's) relationship. I mean, I think our cat could tell that the home itself was against her being there. I would go down to feed her and she would either defiantly walk away or violently scratch me. It was like a kidnapper bringing food to his or her abductee. There was no love there.

The energy at the neighbors' house was decidedly different. There was this air of casualness and controlled disorder. I think it was just that they were "normal." Also, they lacked cynicism—an attribute I admired. I mean, it *was* their country after all. The natural feeling of "I belong" does wonders for people's moods, and they seemed to exude that. For cynical Jews, a defining characteristic can be "I'll never belong, so I'll settle on showing those 'belongers' a thing or two." Maybe I was a little like our cat, but I found a home that didn't mind as much having me around.

I settled into a new routine: I took the bus home from my school, dropped my bag at my house, and then walked down to their house through their sliding door, grabbed a glass of milk, and turned on their TV, waiting for them to come home. It was like a rented family. From our first introduction, this would continue for weeks upon bliss-filled weeks. It was a new milk-fed world, and I relished it.

Often, I would eat dinner there and wander home afterward to my house, happy in the knowledge that I had a new family.

One day, I dropped my bag and walked down to their house, grabbed my glass of milk, and turned on the TV as usual. After about twenty minutes, their front door opened. Typically, it would be the younger daughter, or the son (the one I played catch with), but this time it was two men. They rushed in and ran immediately down the hallway that led to the bedrooms. They didn't see me, as I was in the recliner in the living room holding a glass of milk.

I wasn't sure exactly who they were, but it wasn't my house, so I figured it was better not to ask. After a few minutes, I saw them run out back through the narrow opening that separated the living room from the front hallway. One carried a small television, and the other followed shortly behind. I took a sip of milk.

After a moment, they ran back in to the other side of the house. Again, I sipped my milk. I was confused, but not really rankled yet. A minute passed and they rushed by again. This time one was holding a ceramic box. The other stopped. Our eyes met. I smiled. He called to his companion.

I began to sense a whiff of "I'm going to die." A real primordial intuition. A tangible air of a predator/prey scenario. The first guy rushed back in and stood next to the guy who was glaring at me. Then they both glared. It felt like a long time—us three in a tense stare-down.

Finally, the first guy broke the ice. "Who are you?"

"Jon," I said.

"Stay in the fucking chair," he said.

I nodded. I felt a whit of piss expel into my undies.

"Where are your parents?" he said.

"They're at work," I replied. They looked at each other. "But I don't live here," I said.

"What do you mean, you don't live here?"

"I'm the n-neighbor," I stammered.

"What?" the second guy said.

"I live next door."

"You said your parents were at work."

"They are," I said. "My mom's a dancer." Just a quick plug for the arts. "It's not my house, I swear."

"Where do you live?" he barked.

"That one," I mumbled, pointing through the glass door behind me, at my house.

They looked at each other, flummoxed. It was confusing, but we were working at cross-purposes. It was the first time I realized that sometimes the truth doesn't matter. The first guy walked up to me and stuck his face close to mine.

"Don't move. Don't call the cops. Don't call your parents. If you get up from that chair, we'll kill you." Then he took the TV I was watching and they left.

So I sat there, for about forty minutes, completely still. The daughter came home and found me sitting straight up, holding my half glass of milk like I was displaying it in a milk commercial. I signaled for her to sit. The mother and dog quickly followed. It didn't take long before she saw what had happened. I told her what happened, and then the police came and I gave my statement.

The police asked why I didn't call sooner, and why I didn't get the license number or look for what kind of car they left in. I explained that they threatened to kill me, so I didn't want to die. Look, it was a failure on my part not to act, but I was a kid and I was scared and it would have been extraordinary to have been able to do more.

A week or so later, my house was robbed. As my parents called the police, a flash of the moment when I pointed and said, "That one," crossed my mind.

CHAPTER 5

How I Failed to Do Anything Significant with My Disease

I've always been a rather sick person, in that I get sick a lot. Or I think I do. I'm a bit of a hypochondriac, but not to an extreme. I would classify myself as comfortably hypochondriacal. I once went to the emergency room because I thought a pimple was a spider bite, and that spider eggs were inside my temple, and that when they hatched I would die. Also, maybe I was high on psychedelic mushrooms.

When I was in my early teens, I started getting serious stomach problems. Most people have their first sexual experience then, but I had my first colonoscopy—which is not altogether *not* a sexual experience depending on your proclivities. Some would swoon at the idea of being probed anally. For me, looking back, I recall those years at school as being consumed by crushing anxiety. Anxiety about everything: about talking to others, about performing academically, about budding sexuality, about being short, about understanding my role in school, in life, in everything.

And then I started to bleed from my a-hole. Classic overreaction.

I was diagnosed with colitis, a pretty well-known disease in the pantheon of diseases. But here's the thing: I grew to love this disease. And not that it wasn't a seriously debilitating disease. It was. I'll quickly sketch it out: Thirteen-year-old me would be walking to class with a group of friends and then I would suddenly be overcome with wrenching pain in my abdomen accompanied by the urgent need to shit my pants, so I would buckle over, or "take a knee."

Back then, there were no cell phones to pretend to take a call, so I developed a very extensive inventory of feigns, as in things I could do in the event of a colitis spasm. For instance, I would pretend to tie my shoe or drop a book. If people held up and waited, I would signal for them to go on and I would remain, frozen in a full-body seize, until the cramp would pass or I would shit my pants. Sometimes, this process was almost balletic: I would cramp up, bend over, pause for some time, then move again, only to suddenly re-cramp up moments later, and so on, all across the quad of my junior high school. It was like a game of Red Light/Green Light without anyone playing the stoplight. Because of this, I was late for biology a lot.

But everything became clear in those moments. I found a real and singular purpose: find a bathroom. The ultimate version of this pas seul came much later in my twenties on the second floor of the Kmart at Astor Place in Manhattan. Right as I was about to get on the escalator going down, a cramp hit and I froze up, perfectly positioned about five feet in front of the top of the up escalator. As everyone walked off, I was just standing there in front of them, staring blankly, trying not to evacuate my bowels; but to them, it must have seemed like I was the second-floor greeter.

I was so stuck and mortified that I just began waving hello to each person in an attempt to make it less curious. The face one makes when he is desperately holding in explosive diarrhea is in the general ballpark of a smile. A weird, very forced flat smile. I think it lasted a good fifteen minutes, and I greeted at least thirty or forty Kmart shoppers.

I finally gathered myself to shuffle over to my friend Bill's apartment, who lived relatively nearby in the East Village. And when I reached his bathroom, everything was right in the world and I was alone and at peace.

As I see it now, colitis was not the disease, anxiety was the disease, and colitis was the cure. It was a safe harbor. And with it, I gained the power to be alone. Being alone is a seriously underrated power. An agoraphobic superhero would make a good TV series some day.

I used to get to take long reprieves from the real world when I got bouts. I could miss school, stay at home, and be alone for long periods of time. The only enemy to my disease was remission, and when it came, I would be compelled to return to the grind and go back to school and sit in classes dreaming of some near or far-off time when my colitis would return to me, inflame my intestines, then whisk me home to the safety and security of my bedroom leading to my hallway leading to my bathroom.

Now, with this curse comes great responsibility, and I will say that many people befallen by any number of conditions have done extraordinary things because of their disabilities and ill-health and concomitant solitude. And with them, I could share some filament, some connecting tissue, some common yearning to a more complex understanding of the core of human existence. This time alone with my disease could create space for deeper thought— to cultivate the necessary introspection that spins the dreams of reason. Like Descartes during the winter of 1619, when he sat alone in a room with just a stove and conceived analytical geometry. That could be what my colitis could do for me. I just needed time to wait for the thunderclap of inspiration. And I waited, and I went to the bathroom a lot, and I waited some more.

Descartes is said to have had a series of three dreams during that period, dreams that served as a prophecy, and with that, his life changed. Before the dreams, he was consumed with anxiety and self-doubt, and after the dreams, his purpose was clear and his work took shape, which culminated in *Discourse on the Method*.

I'm trying to remember what I dreamed about in my room when I sat there with colitis. I think it was something like this: I was on a boat, but the boat had my childhood bedroom in it, and in my room I was swaying back and forth, and then I threw up a brown, marshmallowy ball, which stuck to my hands. But my dream, unlike those of Descartes', led to no revelation and no great work to come, just more anxiety and stomach pain. I mean, I still have colitis and still enjoy being alone, and that's my version of analytical geometry.

CHAPTER 6

The Teen Years (or How I Failed Hosting a Bar Mitzvah Party)

Teen years are frequently beset with failure, so I realize it's a gray area for me, because by definition, teens are, on the whole, a hot mess and, as a matter of course, so was I. I have a teenage son right now, and he's mainly an angry cur who eats Cheetos all day and regularly slams doors (not a metaphor). If I left my son home alone with his friends in our apartment for more than fours hours, all the food would be eaten, like *all of it*, including the dry goods; the furniture would be tossed and turned over; and at least one of the kids would have a head injury or worse. And there would be puddles of piss on the bathroom floor. And one of them would have mixed all the available liquids, including cleaning products, together in a bowl along with creams and powders and old paint to try to make a bomb.

Teens are this grisly combination of suppressed rage, sexual confusion, vanity, and unrelenting incompetence, but there may be a redeeming sweetness there, some-where, buried very deep. Just imagine Donald Trump but more agile. Or a turkey vulture. There is a constant war between needing affirmation and shunning affirmation.

My first connection, and many teens' first connections, besides with one another, was with music. So music and friends became this identity Venn diagram, and when I entered the seventh grade, music became a driving factor in how I defined myself and how I was perceived by oth-ers. I can't put my finger on it, or how it all started, but I began to like disco. Honestly, it was not a popular choice among most of the people I knew. Like I previously men-tioned, my father is a jazz fan and my mother was a ballet dancer, so she listens to primarily classical. My sister, at the time, was into folk and folk rock. Her al-bums collection was a lot of Joni Mitchell, Joan Baez, America, Linda Ronstadt, etc. And Worcester was not a welcoming place for disco.

I think it started because I went to visit my friend while he was at theater camp, and I met a girl whose father was the head of Casablanca Records—or a girl lied that her father was the head of Casablanca Records—and she played some records for me, like Donna Summer and "Funkytown," and I believe we kissed. Therefore, I really liked disco.

And disco was a slippery slope. It was a direct line to roller-skating and that was a very dangerous line to draw. Roller rinks were like Planned Parenthood. Kids who hated disco and roller disco would hang out outside roller rinks to jeer at kids who went in. So the one place young disco lovers could gather was heavily targeted by anti-disco mobs.

The main enemy to disco was rock-and-roll fans, or burnouts. Burnouts were thirteen-year-old, pack-a-day smokers who wore denim and only listened to Led Zeppelin and the Rolling Stones, and maybe T. Rex. Double burnouts listened to stadium rock but also dabbled in metal, like Black Sabbath and Judas Priest. The Bruce Springsteen crowd was also squarely anti-disco, and wore less denim (but still quite a bit of denim) and more baseball caps. Burnouts would never wear baseball caps. Even punk was represented, but punk rockers were like the Amish. They weren't missionary. They just hated everybody equally and kept to themselves.

How did one manifest the disco lifestyle from ages twelve to sixteen? The pre-club and pre-cocaine-sniffing demographic of disco listeners? Mainly, buying the 45s and feathering one's hair. Slacks were part of it, but I never really got involved in the fashion. Going full disco was an invitation to bodily harm. Worcester was no Stonewall. Antigay sentiment was rampant. I can't even imagine what it was like growing up gay in central Massachusetts in the seventies, but I had a small taste by liking disco. "Jew fag" was a very popular thing to call me in seventh and eighth grade, and that was primarily by teachers.

Also, I could dance. The capacity to do the disco splits was a big asset to have in the disco community, and because I inherited a little of my mother's dance ability, I could pull off disco splits, including with roller skates on—a real advantage. And that feeling of total confidence within the sacred confines of the rink, with the colored lights flashing and "He's the Greatest Dancer" pulsating and my pulling off a seamless disco split—down and instantly back up. Fucking heaven.

But then came the cold blast of punishing reality leaving the rink, realizing that disco was a hermetic world, roundly hated by the outside world. They didn't want us to roller-dance. They didn't want us to fluidly move our bodies and feel the wind in our heavily sprayed, feathered hair. Look, the bottom line is, disco was not a masculine musical form. I don't think disco was ever used in a war movie—a bunch of soldiers blasting "Ring My Bell" while gearing up for battle.

The negative backlash of my pro-disco stance was pretty harsh. I was punched in the stomach at school by some pointed enemies who were radical in their animosity toward disco. This became a day-to-day issue. One particularly chubby rock supremacist would chase me around school to try and rough me up, but fortunately I was too quick to get caught. Still, it took an emotional toll. At a pizza parlor, I got cornered by two Led Zeppelin lovers. They poured the salt and pepper shakers over my head, threw my sub sandwich on the ground and stepped on it, and said, "Fuck disco."

Another time, my friend Nathan and I biked in the woods to smoke cigarettes, and we made the dubious choice of riding Nathan's mom's tandem bike. We were, unbeknownst to us, followed by a group of kids on dirt bikes who found us in a clearing sitting on a rock, smoking and listening to disco on a transistor radio. Not a great look. They destroyed the bike and the radio and beat us both up. That was a long walk home, carrying that busted-up tandem bike, but that was the price to pay for smoking to disco.

Threats of violence notwithstanding, the silver lining was that disco dancing was a popular pastime at bar mitzvah parties, and because I was a competent dancer, I was at least good at a party. Bar mitzvah parties were also my first foray into sexual experimentation. It was like junior swinging. But because I was "disco," negotiating these parties was treacherous. Most of the kids all attended the same parties, and, therefore, I was an easy target at each and every one. Many of those parties involved a kind of stealth blending in, mixed with a hypervigilance because you never knew when contra forces would strike and just start throwing punches.

This strategy got more and more problematic as parties continued, culminating in a real showdown at the Bancroft ballroom late in the bar mitzvah season. It was a run-of-the-mill party, with all the usual suspects in a hotel ballroom with a DJ playing music and games. I was on the make with a girl in my class when I got word that a disco hater was waiting outside the door, so if and when I left, he was going to kill me. It was like a mob hit, except the mobsters had just finished a Hula-Hoop contest.

There was only one exit; I quickly realized I was trapped. Melancholia set in as I realized what my disco life hath wrought. I wearily contemplated my future, never-ending struggles to live in peace with my syncopated beat and groovy bass lines. But for now, there was just a dark foreboding of a life spent pointing my finger at the sky, then down at the ground in a diagonal motion, repeated again and again, only in the shadows.

So, after feeling too sorry for myself, the party was all but empty, and I was sitting against the wall mired in panic. I think I might have even started to cry. Disco lovers aren't afraid to cry in fear. And then, from above, he appeared.

He was a boy. His name was Chuck, and he had blond hair in a buzz cut that looked slightly white supremacist—he looked like a character out of a photo from the fifties, where he might have been holding a WE WON'T GO TO SCHOOL WITH NEGROES poster. He was unusually large for thirteen.

He said he had heard what was going on and told me he would escort me out. A real *My Bodyguard* moment. I didn't really know him that well, and I wasn't sure why he was helping me, but he had made me an offer I couldn't refuse. I gathered myself and followed him out. He stopped me before the exit and said, "You go first."

I asked, "Why? The kid is out there."

He said, "You'll see."

The kid who was waiting was still there, and as I walked out, he looked at me like an animal that hadn't been fed. He started toward me, and then Chuck came out and walked right between us, almost on cue, abruptly halting the kid's advance. Chuck looked down at the kid and said simply, "Hey."

The kid looked up in soul-crushing defeat. Chuck signaled with his eyes for me to walk on. I don't think I ever felt more vindicated in my life as I walked by that sour kid who rained on my Bancroft bar mitzvah party, who knew in one instant that all that waiting was for naught. I took my time striding by, soaking in my moment. I asked Chuck why he did it, why he helped me, and he quietly said, "I like disco."

My own bar mitzvah party was going to be the best one of the year, for one simple reason: a disco ball. Yes, a disco ball. The sun of the disco solar system. My father, from his lighting supply store, brought one home. It by no means made up for the fact that my party was to be in the basement of my mother's dance studio. But, like I said, I had a disco ball, and how many people have a personal disco ball? Maybe at the Neverland Ranch? Maybe the publisher of *Hustler*'s apartment? Maybe Halston's yacht? Maybe Saddam Hussein's torture room? John Travolta's steam room? Or John Travolta's torture room? Maybe Dennis Hopper's van? Or Gore Vidal's home gym? Possibly Henry Kissinger's man cave?

Anyway, access to party lighting was the first real perk (besides decent housing and education and a YMCA membership) of my father's vocation. He hung it in the center of the room, turned off the lights and tried it out, and suddenly this musty basement became a musty basement splattered with constantly moving patterns of silver light. I stood and paid witness to this otherworldly display, awed by the possibilities of all my secret fantasies realized. A private disco paradise.

My parents had made an agreement to stay upstairs during the party, and they had arranged for the DJ and some snacks and party favors. This was going to be like if Studio 54 and a Hebrew school had a baby. The DJ arrived, and he seemed a little older than the DJs at most of the other parties I had been to, but no bother—the pool of available bar mitzvah DJs in the Worcester area couldn't be that large. He set up some albums and plugged in his equipment while some kids started to arrive.

The small disco light in the center of this beige-painted cinder block room was spinning, and it must have looked like Al Qaeda in the Arabian peninsula was having their holiday party. The DJ started to speak, and he introduced himself to the kids and mentioned he was the afternoon DJ at 14Q, which was the local oldies station. Wait, the DJ was from 14Q? It was the station my parents listened to.

Sinatra came on. Not kidding. "Summer Wind," I believe. Not Earth, Wind & Fire, but "Summer Wind." Kids were confused and milling about. "Summer Wind" played out and seamlessly transitioned into "The Best Is Yet to Come" by Tony Bennett, with a slow, sappy intro from the DJ about my becoming a man. It was clear now my parents had hired an AM oldies DJ. Also, no party games, limbo, musical chairs, or anything, just music from the soundtrack to *Show Boat*. So despite the promise of the disco ball, my bar mitzvah party was more like a wedding at Mar-a-Lago than a kid's disco party.

I politely asked the DJ if he had anything more modern to play, and he pulled out a few albums, like Chicago and John Denver. *John Denver?* Playing John Denver at a bar mitzvah would be like playing the Village People at a funeral, with the key exception of one of the members of the Village People's funeral, in which case it would be more than appropriate to play the Village People. Although it does allow for the possibilities of a "Rocky Mountain Chai" joke (chai the Hebrew symbol, not the tea). . . . But this DJ didn't tell jokes.

The party limped on, with kids standing around to the oldies. Chuck showed up, and I was mortified. He had saved me because of disco, and this was how I repaid him? My disco bodyguard stood there listening to Nat King Cole, looking disappointed. He did give me my favorite gift though: thirteen dollars in one-dollar bills. There was something memorably poignant about that gift. It should be the model for all gifts. I got a lot of silver pen sets and Israeli savings bonds but the thirteen dollars in ones was by far the standout.

Kids started leaving early. Chuck left. The party ended

with me and a few kids in the other room while the DJ played his tunes to the revolving spectral gleam of the disco ball alone until he packed up his gear and left quietly into the AM waves of the night. At least my parents didn't hire a talk radio DJ, although talk radio might have been a little more festive.

CHAPTER 7

Shelves
(or How I Failed to Star in a Pornographic Movie)

My father has a real throbbing work ethic. Can I put it like that? I guess I did, because it was powerful and strong, but at the same time it reverberated. If his work ethic was a sound, it would be a foghorn—nice to hear in the fog and helpful to the safety of fellow travelers, but hard to sleep to.

I have always felt both admiration for and aggravation by his steady dose of principled, hard work. I guess you could say he's the ocean in our volatile post–climate change world, and I'm the seawall. He is a force that, in time, slowly erodes away all that resists. I know that sounds like an insult, but honestly, it's more a tribute. But at best, we worked at cross-purposes. I was the "yawn" to

his yang. To be blunt, he was industrious, and I was sluggish (am sluggish). I like to think that our master/appren-
tice relationship went just sideways, which is at least not
down. Still, he tried.

As mentioned, he owned an electrical supply business,
and that left open many opportunities for me to work
there or help out on weekends, etc. I was a pitiable employee. I was like the Billy Carter of the place, a fun-loving
embarrassment. People liked me, but I was completely
inept at carrying out simple tasks. I broke more bulbs
than I sold and lost many customers by wandering about
the warehouse trying to find inventory without a clue
where it was. Work was like a foreign language to me,
which was all the more curious considering how easily it
came to my father. I was good for a little light conversation and made a relatively easygoing lunch companion,
and I could definitely nap at will.

The ability to snap-nap served me well in future em-
ployment. I remember, once, I took an order at the counter of my dad's store, and the next thing I remember, I
was woken up in a large box on the floor. I had actually
taken an order, started to fill it, then found a box to take
a nap in, never to return to the customer. That pretty
much sums up my work ethic.

My father's ceaseless attempts to right my ship led him
to outsource my services to another company: a friend of
his who ran a fledgling commercial phone-installation

business. This was more likely than not some under-handed Trojan horse–style attack on this man, consider-ing how detrimental I was to my dad's company's bottom line. My task was to build shelves in his new warehouse space to store his cables and wire and other inventory. A big task for a sixteen-year-old with no carpentry skills whatsoever.

The kicker was that I was working alone, with no help or supervision. Supplies were provided, including the lum-ber and tools to make the shelves. I had the whole summer, but time wasn't germane in this practical experiment. It felt more like a thought experiment. Like Schrödinger's cat, but in this case, if a boy is put in a room alone for two months with materials to build shelves with no ability to build shelves, is it only to serve to illustrate how a random subatomic event that may or may not happen in this room or outside renders the point of the task moot, thereby is there even a task at all if it can't be performed, or can there be no task and a task simultaneously?

For about a week, I sat next to a pile of wood and lis-tened to the radio in a state of quasi-suspended anima-tion. I knew I couldn't start, because then I would have to finish, and I knew that would be pointless since I would then have to answer for my work, which would have been definitively not shelves. Better to just wait. I thought maybe I could better explain having done nothing than try to justify the work I would have done. This convoluted logic was something of a comfort to me. And no one ever came around, so I was really in the groove.

After a few weeks, I had moved the wood around a bit and set up something of a model of where the shelves would be. It was more as if a toddler had been told to make shapes out of some wood. A guy who worked for the boss came by and looked at my work thus far and he shockingly gave his approval—a "keep it up."

"So, yeah, I've set up the basic outline of where the shelves will go, and then I'll start building them up, but I'm basically pretty sure I will build with this basic setup, unless it changes, which I doubt, but I want to make sure this plan works best before I really get the shelves up."

"Sounds good, I'll tell Barry."

"Oh yeah, I'm hoping to really get started quickly now that I'm good with the setup."

"Yeah, all right then."

"But based on this, it could change, as in orient this way instead of that way? Right?"

"Yeah, that would work."

"Good, just want to make sure this works best for the shelves, because, you get one shot at this."

"Yup . . . back to work."

"Yeah, me too."

I knew now that stalling was my best quality and best hope for a reasonable excuse for never building anything. An acceptable nonconclusion to this job. So, the plan was as follows: I would keep moving the wood around in different configurations and would keep this up as long as possible. In the event of another supervisor coming by, I would state that I'd changed the plan so as to maximize the best outcome for the shelves. Hopefully this would get me through the next few months. At least, that was the goal. So I went back to listening to the radio and sipping iced tea. Another stretch of time where I was never visited. Just me alone with my wood. And then, one morning, quite early, a van pulled up and changed everything.

A man exited, with ankles shackled, led out of the van by some sort of uniformed guard. Barry, the boss, was there along with a couple of other employees. They signed some paperwork and then he was led over to me.

"This is Jerry Franklin, he's going to be working with you for the rest of the summer."

Jerry was smiling but had no teeth. He appeared to be either in his late twenties or his early fifties. Hard to tell based on the lack of teeth. I shook his hand.

"Jerry is on a work release program from the Walpole penitentiary and he'll be with you till five every day. Jon, show him around and what you're working on and he'll work with you on the project." And that was that. Everyone basically went their separate ways, and there I stood with Jerry from the Walpole prison. You know that feeling when you realize you have to spend an entire summer with a convicted felon? That's how I felt.

The upsides right off: he was very friendly. I'm guessing getting out of jail puts one in a good mood. So chipper he was. And talkative. I had been talking to a pile of wood for the last three weeks, so company was welcomed. Also, the way he talked. Having no teeth makes people sound funny, and he did, like Walter Brennan singing "Old

Rivers." There was a lot of excitable lisping. The last (and for obvious selfish reasons) was that now somebody could actually build the shelves, which was a major relief considering I was increasingly on edge about the inevitable showdown with Barry when I would have had to confess that I couldn't build shelves.

So I took the good with the bad in this case. Jerry had to be good with his hands, right? If you can murder, there's a good shot you're handy. And look, I was not aware he was a murderer, yet, but I was curious, considering I was alone in a warehouse with him surrounded by things to murder with, like hammers and nail guns and saws and screwdrivers and table saws and shovels and wire to strangle with and heavy-duty garbage bags to put me in, etc.

Jerry cased the place and stood around the huge collection of wire on spools, which were accumulating in one corner of the warehouse and the reason the shelves were being built—to store the wire.

"Thatsh a lotta wire."

"Yeah."

"You gosh a car?"

"Umm, yeah?"

"Coolth."

The next day, the prison van pulled up and Jerry bounded out, bound. He looked extra happy. That big gummy smile. I hadn't exactly slept, knowing I was working again with Jerry. He had told me he was in jail on drug charges and "some other stuff," so it was still up in the air what "other stuff" meant.

"Gonna be a bishy day today!"

"Yeah."

Jerry was lanky and strong, and very jumpy, like a puppy. He did have this positive energy, and that cut against my paranoia.

"Can you build shelves?" I asked.

He laughed. "I can't build shit."

"Oh, I assumed you could build, that's why they brought you here."

"No, man, I'm here becush a guy who knoth Barry put in a word for me and he help thet thish up."

"Oh, 'cause I'm supposed to build shelves in here."

"Oh, well I can help."

"I don't know how to build shelves."

"Oh, did you tell them?"

"Not yet, no."

He laughed. "Ain't there nobody 'round here?"

"No, pretty much just me all day every day."

"So you don't do nothin'?"

"Not really."

Jerry laughed hard again. "Thatff thumpthin'."

He looked around.

"Okay, well, here's what we can do."

He led me over to the spools of copper wire and enlisted me to cut small lengths off each spool and put them in a box. Then he instructed me to take the box into my car.

"At lunch, we'll go to the scrap-metal yard."

I didn't question it, and it wasn't like I was going to take some righteous stance to a guy from Walpole who I had to work with all day, every day for the rest of the summer.

"It's just some clippings, we won't get in trouble."

I drove him to the yard and we sold the copper clipping for around six or seven dollars. He was beaming. On the way back, he did the math. Six to seven bucks a day, at around three days a week, so as not to arouse suspicion, would net him close to twenty-five bucks a week, which apparently was a haul in prison. I was hesitant to make this a regular thing.

"Jerry, why don't I give you some money every week, since I get paid, and then we won't do this anymore, since we could get into trouble if we get caught."

"No! Thatff crazy. I ain't taking your money. We gotta earn it."

I didn't really understand the reasoning, but, again, he was in jail for "some other stuff," so I decided not to voice my dissent.

After a few weeks, Jerry and I settled into a pretty comfortable relationship. He was making beaucoup money from his copper scheme and I was enabling his satisfaction. I started to realize that the more he was out of prison, the more I was in prison, doing his bidding every day, buying his lunches and driving him to sell his wire snippets. I was basically his bitch. But just like the majority of prison bitches, I was content as long as the relationship remained uncomplicated.

He regaled me with tales of how he was spending his money in jail. You know, cigarettes and Top Ramen. Very short stories. He was on the rise at Walpole, and I was helping, and he was generous with his praise. So I was abetting a very, very small criminal enterprise and essentially getting nothing out of it. It was like a really anemic *Bronx Tale*. And on top of it all, no shelves. About a week after, Jerry was in an excitable mood, and he said he had big plans for lunch.

"Today we're goin' to my coushin's for lunch."

"What?"

"I spoke to my coushin on the phone and we're gonna go for lunch."

"Okay."

We drove to a three-decker not far from where we worked and walked up a half flight of concrete steps to the ground-floor apartment unit. A woman opened the door and hugged Jerry. He introduced me as we walked into the apartment. She was in tight jean shorts and a tank top and was maybe in her mid-twenties. I don't remember her name, so let's just call her "the cousin."

We stood around for a minute in her kitchen and chatted. There was a smell that was unpleasant, but I was just trying to be polite and process the thought of eating lunch there. There were dirty dishes in the sink and a general vibe of uncleanliness. Jerry then told her to get changed. She went into the bedroom. It was, for sure, a curious moment.

"Are we going out?"

"No. Do you want to fuck her?"

"Ummm . . . uh . . . what?"

"On film?"

"*On film?*"

"Yeah, I shet it allz up."

"Set up *what?*"

"Shet up to record you and her in the bedroom. We made it look like a hotel room."

"Wait, *what?*"

"Yeah, a porno about you and her fucking in a hotel room."

Decent plot, but . . .

"What made you think I would want to do a porn movie?"

"You don't?"

"NO!"

Now the cousin came out wearing a robe.

"He doeshhn't want to do it," Jerry blurted.

"I'm sorry, I didn't realize I was being brought to do this."

I think I had had sex once before, and that can best be described as my penis going into a girl's vagina for a second and a half before I abruptly pulled it out and ejaculated onto my parents' white shag rug. So, now, technically the second time, if agreed on, would be on camera with Jerry from Walpole prison and his cousin. I also didn't know a great deal about the porn industry, but I didn't think it was done on this scale. She handed Jerry a pretied bow tie. Jerry put it on.

"I was going to be the bellhop."

There was a part of me that most certainly was interested in the proposition of doing it. I was sixteen. I was horny often enough without the opportunity of ever doing pornography, and as far as life-changing offers, this was definitely one, whether good or abysmally bad. There were too many questions. Did they have decent distribution? Would I receive an ownership stake? Was the cousin a patient lover? Do people enjoy watching less than three seconds of intercourse? Would this hurt my career opportunities both in and out of pornography?

"Well?"

"So what happens?"

"I show you into the room as a bellhop, holding this bottle of champagne, and you two go fuck on the bed."

The cousin stared out blankly as if pondering her character's motivation. It was a deceivingly simple story line. Couple goes to a hotel room. So many title possibilities. *HO-tel, Motel 69, The Cummer's Suite, A Room with a Jew, Turn-On Service, Go-Down Service, Dial B for Boner* (I know that's not technically hotel-related but I like it). I looked at Jerry with his bow tie hanging loosely over his dirty T-shirt and his come-hither-and-fuck-my-cousin grin, and I had a real thought to do it, if only for Jerry. I mean, I pretty much did everything for him. And what were the consequences if I said no? Would Jerry kill me because I wouldn't have sex with his cousin? I was beginning to enter my Danger Zone: that place where I need a paper bag to breathe into, so as not to keel over. I said the first thing I could think of.

"I'll be the bellhop."

I realized only after I sputtered this out, the ramifications of this. In essence, it involved a cute way out for me, but via a wildly unorthodox scenario: Jerry fucks his cousin. When I realized what I'd suggested, I became even more tense, as in, was he going to kill me for even floating the idea of incest on tape? He looked over at his cousin, and she looked at him. There was no "light bulb" moment, but they did look at each other for an extended amount of time.

Twenty minutes later, I entered the cousin's bedroom with a pre-tied bow tie around my neck and delivered the line, "Your champagne, sir." An hour after that, I was back at the warehouse with Jerry, sitting next to a pile of wood, listening to the radio.

We never finished the shelves. We tried. We built a portion of them. I hope they kept them, because they were more public art than shelves. Jerry got in the van that last day of our job and he turned around and smiled and waved. Even though he fucked his cousin, I knew I would miss him. In any event, it was shot on Beta and it's out there somewhere. If any of you readers are die-hard porn aficionados, keep your eyes peeled for the sixteen-year-old bellhop.

CHAPTER 8

The Threesome
(or How I Failed to Quantify It)

There are different kinds of ménage à trois experiences. To be brief, I'll break them down into three categories. The "intellectual threesome," the "classic threesome," and the "Benjamin threesome." For the intellectual threesome, Carl Jung and his wife, Emma, and Toni Wolff serve as a prime example. Wolff was a student of Jung's and became his lover. The relationship took place over several decades and became deeply personal and involved. It was, as I understand, primarily sexual to start but it evolved into a binding, evocative, and complex triad that fueled both discord and intellectual rigor. The "classic threesome" is more immediate and short-lived and involves, as a matter of course, clear liquor and lube. "The Benjamin threesome" is altogether unique.

Threesomes are not always smooth. Or at least, mine

wasn't. For some people, threesomes are natural. I've talked to people who speak of them like they are not awkward at all. Like, "Hey, I hooked up with these two girls last night and it was totally sweet," or "I met these two guys at a bar and we went back to my place and went at it," or "When I was in Canada, I had a threesome with this member of the House of Commons and his wife." I bristle at sexual openness and easygoing attitudes.

For me, sex has always been an intensely anxiety-provoking proposition. Maybe it was the way I was raised: feral by wolves—wild, heathen sex wolves. Watching those wild wolves go at it all night and day can affect a child's disposition on sexual mores. Sex is, admittedly, problematic for a lot of people, so I'm not a total anomaly. I'm a second-guesser when it comes to sexual behavior. There're a lot of fits and starts with me. Like, fussing about and excusing myself a lot to go to the bathroom. It may just be a general lack of confidence, but is this turning you on?

I remember the first time a girl reached down my pants, in the basement of my house, I seized up so fast, I thought my appendix had burst. It took like three weeks for the pain to go away. It was like the devil himself had stuck his pitchfork into my spleen to teach me to not be touched there. Like the ladies used to say to me, "You're a real Johnny Cotton in the sack."

Although, I have made slight progress over the years. Intimacy is not my strong suit, but I've learned to work with the tools I have. As you can imagine, I'm not particularly adventurous. Even missionary is a bit much for me. My first trip to a porn theater resulted in me throwing out my shoes after, because I thought they may give me gonorrhea, just from the floor.

Part of this may be a product of genetic behavior, as in some people are more sexually open than others. Or it may have been a product of that one time, in eighth grade, during a JV basketball game when I was subbed into the game and got a spontaneous erection. A big moment for me (finally getting to play in a game), and a devastating and curious response (my public erection). It was the saddest time-out ever called. Of course, the backlash was spectacular, with the entire school giving me the time-out gesture for the rest of the year wherever I went.

I attended a small New England college—you know, the one with stone buildings and the obligatory all-white student population. Except for that one kid. Actually, my roommate my first year was one of the very few Hispanic kids on campus, and, simply by random selection, I was introduced, in a deeper sense, to a completely different culture than mine. He was from Spanish Harlem, and I learned so much from him, including how to press Jordache jeans as well as a completist familiarity with "the Roxanne Wars." He also introduced me to systemic racism, and I got to see it, almost every day, unfurl before my eyes. The most revealing part was that he loved it there. This was, to me, a confusing reaction, but it was his way. "Making the best of things" is not a quality of the privileged class.

Freshman year in college was predominately an experiment in poorly mixed cocktails and clumsy sexual liaisons with a sprinkle of astronomy and Victorian literature. The most awkward feature of most sexual encounters, at least in my dorm room, was that they were performed not by me but in my presence by my roommate. There's no better ambient aural experience than to fall asleep to other people fucking. It was such sweet relief to hear it end. And just as the room became quiet in that postcoital glow, and I was finally ready to let sleep take me, they would start up again. My roommate had real stamina. I even think we had a conversation about negotiating down the amount of times he could have repeated sex in the room with me in there, like "It's okay to have it, but can you try to have it no more than twice? I have a nine a.m. lecture."

Also, maybe I'm an old-fashioned sort, but sex should be between a man and a woman . . . or a woman and a woman, or a man and a man, or a man and a doll, but not *in front* of a man or a woman. I considered going the *It Happened One Night* route and putting up a sheet, but then I would've also needed sound baffling. But this was the general nature of college sexual behavior. It was a bit circus-like, in that people would have sex like elephants, as in anywhere they could at any time, with no trainer to whip them to stop.

As an upperclassman, I lived in a prison cell–size concrete-block dorm room with a Cure poster and a mini fridge. A guy down the hall was a strapping guy who played on the college soccer team. He was handsome, charming, athletic, a smooth talker and an all-around popular type. I had none of his magnetism. One night, he brought in a girl from another dorm and we sat around, chatting and drinking.

The conversation quickly drifted to sex, and he rather blithely proposed that the three of us all have it. This suggestion was like a shotgun got rung off next to my ear. Fortunately, she, like me, seemed not interested. But he was persistent and began this long, inspiring stump speech in favor of group sex. He went on and on about doing things that are memorable and extraordinary . . . and that we wouldn't regret this choice but rather would celebrate it later as an emblem of free spirit, and moments like this should never be left undone. He was like the "threesome wrangler." And how many times had he delivered that speech? It was way too polished to have been extemporaneous. I was nervously giggling a lot and was at least comforted by her expression, which was a mix of "Nice try" and "Holy shit, what a creep."

Then there was a pause, and she looked at us and said very plainly, "I'll go put in my diaphragm." She quickly exited. Stunning development. He casually started undressing with just me in the room. I started to flop sweat. Deep panic. He was suddenly in just his underwear, and I was pacing back and forth like a barrister, prattling on about why we shouldn't do this. He was pretty unfazed by my nervous breakdown. I just hoped she would never come back. Then, a knock. She entered. Fuck!

She looked him over, and they started kissing. He led her to my bed and gestured for me to come over. I complied like an old dog when its owner snaps, slowly loping over toward the bed. He took her shirt off, and I sat awkwardly at the edge of the bed and started stroking her torso like it was a snapping turtle.

Reluctantly, I lay down next to her and took off my shirt. It was like I had rigor mortis. They were quickly naked and stacked on top of each other, and I was half off the bed, looking at the ceiling, trying to conjure invisibility. Soon enough, they were having sex and less and less remembered I was there. For a good fifteen minutes, I tried to make myself as small and inconspicuous as possible while pressed against two people making love in different positions. It was the porn version of the movie *Ghost*. I remember, after "we" finished, putting on my shirt and saying that I should shower.

So, there was born "the Benjamin threesome," technically a twosome with a twist. Or like Canadian doubles, if one person didn't have a racket. My threesome happened fairly spontaneously, but there is a praxis for general application. Just get three people and have one casually observe any two from very close range.

Failed

Sexual

Positions

THE INVERTED JENNY (OR THE JAME GUMB): Lay flat while the man lays atop faceup and smooshes genitals between his legs all the way back to allow awkward and shallow penetration.

THE VEGAN BRUNCH: Cowgirl positioning, but the man cups the penis to his stomach and penetrates as best he can using testicles only.

THE IRAN-CONTRA: Essentially reverse cowgirl, but instead of using your penis, secretly replace with thumb, intensifying the duplicity of the experience.

THE IRAN-CONTRA (WITH THE OLLIE NORTH): Same as the Iran-Contra, but replace your thumb with someone else's.

THE THINKER: One lies flat on the edge of the bed while the other mounts from the top, facing out, in sitting position, with one arm resting on the chin, appearing bored.

THE GARLIC PRESS (OR NEWTON'S REVENGE): From a standing or supine position, hold your partner, crotch to head, while he/she hangs down the buckside, butthole to face, for oral.

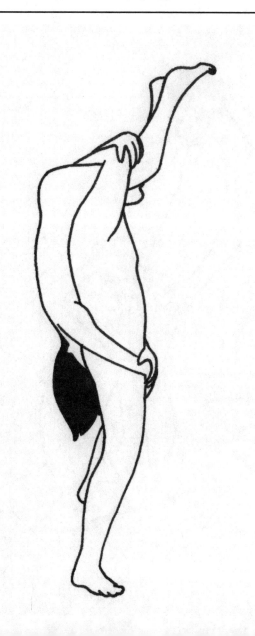

THE WILLIAM TELL: Place your genitals in the hair of your partner and gently grind back and forth until climax.

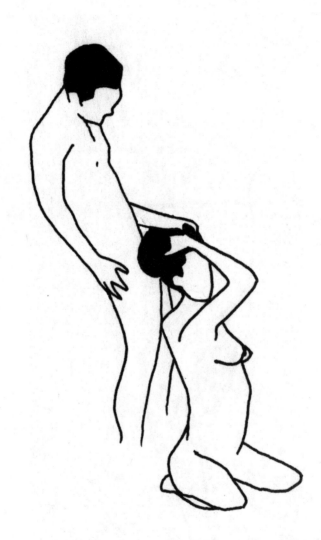

FAILURE IS AN OPTION

THE PATTON: Basic doggy-style, but wearing a sidearm in a holster.

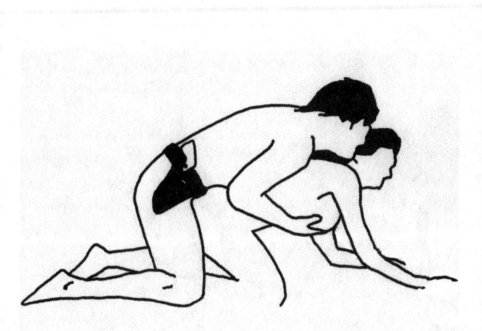

THE CANTANKEROUS COACH: Place pillows behind your back and sit on the bed. She then sits on your lap. As she thrusts back and forth, cross your arms and grimace.

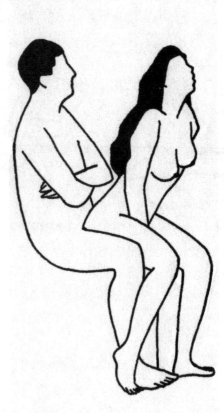

THE VERTIGO: Lie on your back and she straddles you. Assist by grabbing her buttocks and lifting and bouncing. Once she starts to ride up and down at a rhythmic pace, wave your arms and legs in circular motions, creating the optical illusion that you are falling.

THE LAFFER CURVE: The woman (or man), facedown, lifts the body up, arching the back into a reverse U shape, then economist Arthur Laffer has sex with him/her.

CHAPTER 9

How I Failed to Provide a Historical Example of Failure

O kay, so I feel like we are at the point in the book where we need to get serious about the principles of failure from a less anecdotal perspective and get to something more objective. This would obviously require more specific examples of failure in history and how we can use those examples to better understand the nature of failure. But, because I don't have the tools to provide you with any actual careful historical analysis, I decided to reach out to a professional historian so as to cite pertinent examples. This benefits both of us, because we can learn together. Instead of characterizing his research, I will just share our correspondence. This will be the best way to get the full benefit of a more analytical approach to failure. I reached out to classics professor from NYU Andrew Monson.*

Andrew,

I know this is a bit out of the blue, but I am writing a comedy book about personal failure for Dutton, and I wanted to reach out to see if you could take some time to discuss a particular person from antiquity, Roman or otherwise, who personifies failure. It would preferably be someone not well-known, so I can tell their story for a segment in the book. Any chance we could get in touch? Or perhaps you could steer me to someone who could help? Thanks for your time.

H. Jon Benjamin

Dear Jon,

There was a recent book arguing that Alexander the Great was a great failure, but that, of course, deliberately runs counter to what he personifies to most people and he's by no means a poorly known figure; he was too obsessed with

* Yes, I really did contact Andrew Monson, and this exchange really happened. However, our conversation has been slightly modified to enhance failure.

drinking and conspiracy theories to secure his empire. It's hard to think of anyone who, at the same time, sticks out as a personification of failure and is poorly known: the Roman agrarian reformers failed (Tiberius and Gaius Gracchus, and the late Roman emperors failed to keep out the Germanic invaders; some of the Macedonian kings in the dynasty of Cleopatra were ridiculed in antiquity and blamed for Egypt's downfall). I have a hunch you might be looking for a literary character, and, being a historian, I'm perhaps not the best person to ask.

Best wishes,
Andrew

Andrew,

Thanks for getting back. Is there a pivotal moment where someone, by not acting, caused a sea change in politics or jeopardized the stability of the empire or republic? I know this is a very general question, but just trying to pin down for clarity what I'm going for. It can be a historic figure who failed in a big way, in one moment, as opposed to looking at it from a whole career perspective.

Jon

Dear Jon,

I would like to help, but my teaching and research schedule leaves me little time. Good luck with the book and hopefully you can find someone to help with your endeavor.

Best,
Andrew

Andrew,

Again, thanks for getting back. I don't mean to keep pestering, but I do have a whole section of a book to write and deadlines are piling up. I realize you are busy, but I figure you must have, at minimum, one example so I can pass that on to my readers. Thanks again for the time.

Jon

Dear Jon,

There are numerous books on the subject that can provide you a broad array of examples. I would suggest perhaps taking a look at some more comprehensive studies, to give you a sense of the history and the characters who drove it, and that may pay dividends in finding a subject. Depending on your interests and how familiar you are with Roman history, you could pick a few from among:

The Fall of the Roman Republic
by David Shotter

Provides a brief overview of the events leading up to the fall of the republic.

Outlines of Roman History
by William C. Morey

Another brief overview.

History of Rome
by Michael Grant

Popular narrative.

Rome in the Late Republic
by Mary Beard and Michael Crawford

Short overview. Often used in college courses in the United Kingdom.

The Romans: From Village to Empire
by Mary T. Boatwright et al.

This is a commonly used college text in the United States.

A History of the Roman People
by Allen Ward et al.

Another commonly used college text.

The Roman Revolution
by Ronald Syme

Seminal and one of the most influential works, but don't start here.

The Last Generation of the Roman Republic
by Erich S. Gruen

Controversial work directed at Syme.

   I found H. H. Scullard's *From the Gracchi to Nero* impossibly soporific and dull. And [Edward] Gibbon, although enjoyable enough, would probably lead you astray, as his history is really more of an indictment of Christianity than anything else. In other words, Gibbon is not the place to start to learn Roman history. It reads more like a polemic than history (more Voltaire than Michelet).

Best,
Andrew

Dear Andrew,

Look, I don't have time to read any of these. And to be honest, I'm just looking for you to write four to five pages of the book to provide an example for my readers. There are a lot of failures out there who are counting on some historical background, and I don't want to get prickly, but maybe I should have been more direct earlier on what I needed. Can you at least write a few paragraphs on any subject you pick, and I'll just add some stuff to extend it to five pages? I assume you're good at this kind of thing.

Jon

Jon,

I can't just provide you material for your book. It would be a breach of ethics. As I stated, I believe it would be best to get in touch with someone else.

Best,
Andrew

Andrew,

You were the only one to write back. I wrote a bunch of classics professors, and none have

returned my emails. I'm not going to lie,
it would be easier if you wrote something,
and I will credit you in the book and that way,
we would be clear of any ethical questions.
It would be a huuuuuuuuge help. Thanks.
Maybe that agrarian reformer, Gaius Gracchus.
Maybe him?

Jon

Dear Jon,

Please cease contact with me in regards to this
matter.

Best,
Andrew

CHAPTER 10

Dee Har
(or How I Failed to
Move to France)

I love the movie *Five Easy Pieces*.

Let me backtrack. I am pretentious.

When I was in college, I read Camus, but I didn't really understand him. I just knew he was one of those authors deep thinkers would appreciate. Existentialism, as a philosophical movement, was a wellspring for pretentioneers like me. It was because its emblem was nonverbal brooding, so discourse could be avoided—i.e., I rarely had to back it up. I was so bad at branding that my version of being an existentialist was forcing myself to read *The Stranger* and reading the first forty pages of *The Plague*.

And then, the real pièce de résistance (classic pretentious move to overuse French idioms): buying a Camus

T-shirt. I mean, that is real Mall of America–level existentialism. I didn't even have the balls to don a beret or wear all black or smoke a pipe—just a red T-shirt with Camus's face on it. And the problem was, there's a built-in conflict in wearing the Camus T-shirt, because, at the most basic level, the T-shirt is an invitation for like-minded Camus fans to spot me and then spark a dialogue. And this is the real enemy of the pretentioneer: real, deep, meaningful conversation on the topic they pretend to embrace. The hope was, at best, to meet people with no interest in Camus who I could at least establish a false sense of superiority over and then go from there. Sample dialogue as follows:

> **Girl:** (*Pointing at T-shirt.*) Who's that?
> **Me:** Oh, it's my favorite author, Albert (*pronounced Al-Bear*) Camus.
> **Girl:** Oh.
> **Me:** Yeah, have you read *The Stranger*?
> **Girl:** No.
> **Me:** Oh, you have to. It's essential existentialism.
> **Girl:** Cool.
> **Me:** I am an existentialist, basically . . . I mean, that feeling of being totally autonomous, untethered. It is that all-encompassing feeling of pure dread and pure freedom, feeding off each other. It's about being totally self-aware and totally authentic. I hate

people who can't see that our natural
state of being is being totally alone the
universe.

Girl: Right . . .

Me: So, do you want to hang out sometime?

After I left school, in 1989, I decided I wanted to move
to France—the ultimate pretentioneer power move. Fake
it till you really fake it. Without that feeling of disconnect-
edness to my world, the move was largely the fulfillment
of what the Camus shirt had done on a small scale. I was
getting serious about my pretentiousness and putting my
money where my mouth was.

So, with that in mind, I asked my parents to pay for it.
Appropriately, they refused, so I took a job at my father's
store and a side job at a chain restaurant in Worcester
called Charley's Eating & Drinking Saloon, home of the
sizzling fajita. In a somewhat related failure, my stint at
Charley's saloon only lasted a few months because of my
sincere inability to deliver the fajitas sizzling, which was
the whole raison d'être (did it again) of the sizzling fajita.

I mainly delivered them non-sizzling due to my se-
verely slow reaction time. The sizzle was created by the
cook hitting the pile of meat and peppers with hot oil
while the plate sat on the expedite counter, and the waiters were meant to swoop in and rush them to the tables.
Here's a snippet of a conversation between myself and the
manager that would commonly occur due to overtly poor
fajita-serving aptitude.

Manager: How do we deliver the fajita?

Me: Sizzling.

Manager: Right. Do we ever deliver a fajita that's not sizzling?

Me: No.

Manager: What happens when a fajita is not sizzling?

Me: We bring them back.

Manager: And whose salary does that come out of?

Me: Mine.

Manager: Right. But what never happens?

Me: The fajita isn't sizzling.

Manager: Yes! The fajitas are never not sizzling when they hit the table!

And after many non-sizzles, the following:

Manager: What's going on?

Me: Nothing.

Manager: How many fajitas have you delivered in the last week?

Me: Fifty, maybe?

Manager: And how many were sizzling?

Me: Most of them.

Manager: Practically none of them.

Me: Umm, I don't think so . . .

Manager: I think so, because I'm the one who gets the complaints.

Me: Maybe they're not smoking real good when I drop some, but there is definitely sizzle.

Manager: What did I tell you when you started here?

Me: Deliver the fajitas sizzling.

Manager: Charley's is known for their sizzling fajitas. That's what works. People come here from all over the area to enjoy them.

Me: Right.

Manager: Deliver them sizzling.

I was on borrowed time from the beginning at Charley's. I just wasn't fast enough, hungry enough, "in it to win it" enough. But I raised enough to buy a ticket to Paris, with money left over to last a good month. I would be like Hemingway, but instead of hooking up with Gertrude Stein, James Joyce, and Picasso, my sole contact was a friend of my aunt Marion's who owned a knickknack shop—more last generation than lost generation. Although, my aunt was a wonderfully eccentric woman who traveled a lot, so my hope was that her contact might prove interesting.

I boarded my one-way flight with big hopes of leaving all that broken America had brought me to live out my days wandering the streets and parks of Paris, a true bohemian.

After taking the Metro into the city, I had the address of the hotel I had booked for the first few nights before I had to hustle an apartment or long-term place to stay. When I arrived, it was late at night, and the matron of the hotel spoke no English and had no record of my reservation and no rooms available, so I was out on the street to fend for myself. But this is what I wanted, right? A true Parisian bohemian experience. Nowhere to sleep, with only thousands of American dollars in my pocket.

So, I called home and cried. My rocky start did at least fit with my *Moveable Feast*–type plan to live in Paris and embrace my ennui. Embracing one's ennui is a real pretentious to-do. Sullenly walking the streets of Paris would be the postcard view into my faux-tortured soul. The second day, it even rained! Next, visit the American bookstore and buy Parisian poetry, preferably obscure, so I had it at the ready. More wandering the wet streets without an umbrella. Umbrellas are for people who have a place to be. I had no reason not to be wet. Again, totally existentialist.

That night, I made the ill-fated choice to go to an American-themed bar called Tennessee, which was decorated eerily similar to Charley's Eating & Drinking Saloon. It was pretty quiet, and they played country music, and I sat at the bar, with my wet copy of *Les Fleurs du mal*, ready for action. After about an hour, a young man sidled up next to me. He was tall, wiry, and very handsome, like a Jean-Paul Belmondo with long hair. He looked at me and his expression turned to shock.

"Ohhhhh."

I was confused. I assumed he was reacting to my being rain-soaked.

"Broo WHEEL-us," he shouted.

"Umm . . ."

"Broo Wheelus—*DEE Har!*"

"Um, I don't speak French."

"*Mon Dieu!* Broo Wheelus! *Dee Har!*"

"Ummm . . ."

"*Vous etes* Broo Wheelus."

I just nodded.

"Ahhhhh . . . *c'est fou! Dee Har* . . . Jean McClane!"

He was patting me on the back and sputtering drunkenly.

"Jean McClane! Jean McClane!"

His visage changed and he quickly lit a cigarette and then he squinted his eyes and curled his lips and brought a finger up to his mouth and blew on it like a smoking gun.

"Happy trails, Hans."

Then he laughed, loud. And, it became clear to me he thought I was Bruce Willis. I do slightly resemble Bruce Willis. Well, my hairline resembled Bruce Willis's hairline.

He then spoke to the bartender in French, telling him that I was Bruce Willis. Because it had gone this far, I just decided to be Bruce Willis, so I curled my mouth and said, "Welcome to the party, pal," or "Yippee ki yay," or some such line from *Dee Har*. It made more sense, given the language barrier, just to be Bruce Willis than try to explain that I wasn't him. Plus, he was so excited; I didn't really want to kill his dream of having met the real Bruce Willis.

We sat for at least an hour at that bar, where the

bartender clumsily translated for us, and I made up a story about how I was filming a movie in Paris and made up more stories about the set of *Die Hard* and the practical jokes I used to play on Alan Rickman. After some time, I told the bartender to tell him that I needed to go to bed because of an early call in the morning. The bartender relayed back that the man wanted to invite me over to his flat nearby because he was a young actor and wanted to party more with Bruce Willis. I politely declined. I was Bruce Willis, after all. I don't hang out with fans.

We left together and stood out in front of Tennessee, preparing to part ways—the belle epoque streetlamps splashing soft light onto the cobblestone street. I gave him the thumbs-up, and he shook my hand with a firm grip. Our eyes met—my signature Bruce Willis glare and his drunken, watery eyes. And then he pulled me toward him and kissed me long and hard on the lips. I wasn't expecting it, so I didn't quite kiss back, but I was surprised enough to let the kiss last at least ten seconds. It was my first passionate man-on-man kiss. I finally pulled away and awkwardly smiled. He looked at me, as if to say, "Come home with me."

And for one long moment, the thought crossed my mind to let him have me, for one night, just so there would be some random young French actor out there who would have spent the rest of his life telling everyone he knows that he fucked Bruce Willis when he was in town filming a movie. But alas, I turned and walked away. He'll always have that kiss.

So, back to *Five Easy Pieces*. The 1970 film explores the story of an upper-middle-class family whose paterfamilias is a domineering professional classical musician. Jack Nicholson plays his son, who has fled his familial ties by rejecting his music pedigree, becoming a manual laborer/drifter, working on oil rigs and drinking heavily and basically squandering his future. It was essential existential fare, in the tradition of the French new wave. I guess I realize now that I related to it then because I was living out my own version of this story, but in place of wasting my musical genius and working oil rigs, I was just a failed fajita deliverer, staying at student housing.

But now I was in Paris. Maybe technically not as romantic as Nicholson's character, but I was pretentious, so the bar was lowered. In fact, there was even a revival theater in the Left Bank that exclusively showed *Five Easy Pieces*. I would often go see it just to solidify my expat cred. So many levels of irony going on. My rebellion was moving to Paris to watch the same movie over and over about somebody else's rebellion.

As my money started to run dry, about a week and a half in, things got a little desperate. I had moved to a rented flat in the projects of the Stalingrad neighborhood of Paris, which was mostly immigrant (Algerian) and poor. It was like a riches-to-rags story sped up to ten days. If only I was defter at delivering fajitas, I would have had more money. But this quickly became the most thrilling part of my trip. Mainly because the people there were the friendliest, even the hardened criminals.

One guy, after stalking me for a block or so, on my way home, came up behind me. I was certain he was going to rob me, and he said in broken English, "You think I'm going to take your money?" I stared. He laughed loudly. "I would have done that by now, but you live here with us and we don't steal from us. Why steal from the poor? We steal from other neighborhoods, where the money is." That was a relief, and a good rule to live by.

My life in Paris was, at this point, more retired postal worker than young bon vivant/flaneur (again with the French?!). I would sit in the park during the day, then, around four, go to the supermarket and return home to cook a depressing dinner alone in my apartment at night. In a weird way, this was probably the closest to the life of a real artist I'd ever get, except of course for the not-creating-any-art part. It was solitary. But my eye was still on the prize—that is, this was all just the seedbed for the real payoff, which was: "Yeah, I lived in Paris in the late eighties." And also my answer to the question "Oh, what did you do there?"—I'd be able to softly chortle and reply, "What does one do in Paris? *Nothing.*"

Sorely out of funds, I used my aunt's contact to try to get some work from the woman who owned the knick-knack shop, but unfortunately she had no openings selling plastic Eiffel Towers. But she did have a contact in the South of France who ran a commune/farm, which took in volunteers to help with the farming. It was really my only option, so I took it.

I took a train down to a rural area in the Ardèche mountains, where I was greeted by a large American woman, her very small French farmer husband, and their two daughters. The farmer spoke no English and barely any French. He mainly communicated in a series of grunts and slugs from a wine bottle. He looked really "of the earth," almost half human, half botanical, or better described as like a sentient root—a "froot," so to speak.

Their farm surrounded a beautiful sixteenth-century stone house built onto a steep hillside, with tiered bean fields carved into the hill below. They led me to my room in an adjoining shedlike structure with a private small bedroom. Before I knew it, I was summoned to the side of the house, where I met some of the other people who were staying there. Without a moment to even process, the farmer, ax in hand, grabbed a rooster from the yard, strode up to me, and put it in my hand—the ax, not the rooster. He then walked to a tree stump that had a hook fastened in it and jammed the rooster's head under the hook, trapping it. I had not really seen much animal cruelty before, so this was a bit of a shock. He signaled for me to come over and nodded to chop the rooster's head off. Everyone was gathered around, but I just got there and didn't want to immediately murder a bird. Seriously, what the fuck?

The American woman said, "Just aim below the hook

and give it a good swing. All our new guests do it, and tonight we'll make coq au vin to welcome you."

But this felt not altogether welcoming. I got shaky, and I tried to hand the ax back to the farmer, but he looked at me sternly, as if to say, "You will kill it." I had never killed anything before, with the exception of my neighbor's dog, but that was just because I put vodka in its water dish (also, I'm not sure that's how she died. It might have been old age, or vodka). I was really beginning to fall apart now, and the rooster was squirming violently under the hook, and these people were staring at me, so I quickly did a very broad "No, thanks" gesture.

"I don't really kill things," I said. (Replace *We* for *I* and *always* for *really* and you have a potentially good slogan for the army.)

The farmer grabbed my arm firmly, and before I knew it, swung my hands up, guiding the ax above my head, and then forced it down onto the rooster, chopping its head clean off. It happened so fast; I had no course of resistance. I had killed. Well, he had killed. Well, we had killed.

I think it might have been Ted Nugent who claimed that meat tastes all the sweeter if you are the one who's done the killing. As I ate my coq au vin that night, it really tasted pretty much the same as if I hadn't been the rooster killer who cut its head off. Lesson learned.

Around five the next morning, I was awoken by hard poking into my rib cage. The farmer stood there with his dog by his side, stone-faced. He signaled to get up. Tired and disoriented, I quickly dressed. I followed him to his truck and got in. We drove in silence, as the sun peeked over the hill, spreading bright morning light onto the plateaus and deep-cut valleys.

We drove to town and then parked in front of a small café. Inside, we sat and the farmer spoke briefly with the man behind the counter. My head throbbed from the wine from the night before. The man slammed a bottle of wine onto the table, like a sommelier from the Old West. So we sat and drank the bottle in silence. This was my first wine-only breakfast, and it did make me feel a little better, especially considering the "we can't talk, so we might as well drink" vibe, but sunrise is a tad early for booze, I think.

Around 6:30 a.m., drunk, I was dropped in a bean field to pick beans alone in the summer sun. Then, at around noon, already with a hangover from breakfast, the farmer picked me up in his truck with his dog, and we went back to the same café for more wine. More wine? This farmer's tolerance for drinking and bean picking was epic.

At around five thirty the next morning, I felt a poke, and it began again. Back to the café for *vin rouge* at daybreak. Holy fuck! How is this sustainable? By nightfall, I'd aged thirty years. And with dinner came way more wine, and the sorting of the beans into piles small, medium, and large, to be separated for the market. It was literally drink, farm, drink, sleep. Day bled into day, because it had been two days. But by day three, my body was breaking down. *Mon dieu*, the wine.

This was it, my *Five Easy Pieces* moment. Would I commit to my pretentiousness and eschew American upper-middle-class values forever and stay till my liver became large and French, like a swollen leather canteen?

The next day I took a train back to Paris and flew home. As it turns out, even pretentioneers can fail.

Failed Pickup Lines

I couldn't help noticing that you might have social anxiety.

Do you work out, or are you just naturally tense?

Has anyone ever told you you look like my mother?

I've been waiting all my life to ruin this moment.

Excuse me, but is this pussy taken? (*Point at her crotch.*)

Am I seeing double, or do you have two tits?

Are you into double entendres? Because if so, can I look under the mat for the key, so I can open the back door?

I'm an atheist, but after seeing you (*at the top of your lungs*), *Allahu Akbar*!

I know this might sound old-fashioned, but do you want to have sex with me in a cave?

It seems like you have a head for business, and a bod for . . . business. I guess you seem like you're probably in business?

You look exactly like a model . . . who I used to have sex with.

Is it just me, or are you Jewish?

My mother always told me to find a nice girl to "settle for."

I know you've probably heard this before but . . .
 You're a grand old flag,
 You're a high-flying flag
 And forever in peace may you wave.
 You're the emblem of
 The land I love.
 The home of the free and the brave.
 Ev'ry heart beats true
 'neath the red, white, and blue,
 Where there's never a boast or brag.
 Should auld acquaintance be forgot,
 Keep your eye on the grand old flag.

CHAPTER 11

How I Failed to Study
the Holocaust

They say "Those who can't do, teach," but one could also say "Those who can't do, write." I think I'm exposing the veracity of this as we speak, or more accurately, "Those who can't write, still write." Another truism you might entertain is, "If at first you don't succeed, try, try again," but this one has some very dark undercurrents, because if you're Hitler, for example, try, trying again is a bad thing. One would have compelled him to stop trying, because succeeding had some very dire consequences.

The ancient art of tai chi tells us to stop trying, to give ourselves completely to the energy of the universe, because trying is working against a natural flow. I tried this once in an actual fight at the Dream Machine arcade in 1982, and I couldn't stop the fist that was hitting my cheek with my mind, so this model doesn't always work in a practical sense. But there is something very affirming about not try-ing. Professional athletes talk about "the zone," that feeling one gets in the heat of competition, where things basically become effortless, like intuition takes over and all tension is released and they can just "do," instead of "trying to do."

After college, I was trying to do a lot of things, like the aforementioned moving to France to become a socialist farmer, but finally landed on going to graduate school in Chicago for Holocaust studies, to start the process of be-coming a teacher. But it also concurrently set in motion the question of what happens to those who can not only *not do*, but can't even teach. Maybe "Those who can't teach . . . go into real estate"? Or "Those who can't teach, become hobbyist inventors of a food product called 'Vam-pagels: the bagels with two holes,'" or something like that. But at least I was starting to try to become a teacher, even though "trying," as I tried to explain earlier, is against nature. In the late eighties, Holocaust studies was a pretty under-the-radar field of study.

Of course, scholars existed who wrote extensively on the Holocaust, but very few universities actually offered whole programs focused exclusively on it. In fact, I was the only student at the university in the program. So, yes, I was on the ground floor on what would become a real cottage industry, but the downside was a lot of attention was put on me. Being the only student in a program is a bit like being a prince or princess. Everything you do comes under heavy scrutiny. I started to notice this early on, when I turned in my first paper to my professor on the topic of the authoritarian personality in the context of the rise of Hitler, and he wrote across the top: "Grossly insufficient analysis." I blame the heavy scrutiny. He blamed my substandard work. Soon, I would learn that I was very good at "grossly insufficient analysis." In fact, if I were to start an analytics company, I would now call it Grossly Insufficient Analytics.

So it was very quickly established both that I was the sole representative of the Holocaust studies program and that I completely sucked at Holocaust studies. I even attended the inaugural Holocaust studies conference on behalf of my department, where historians spoke on different topics, and I was so woefully underwhelming that I'm pretty sure Elie Wiesel, the keynote, rolled his eyes at me. A few months in, the director of the department brought me in and asked if I was interested in moving into the religious studies department because maybe my "talents" were more suited to that. My own department was trying to trade me to another just to save face. And I was the only one in it. What I lacked was, to put it simply, "academic rigor." I lacked the facility to find hard truths. I couldn't hold firm historical data. I couldn't maintain a heuristic erection. I just couldn't "never forget" it up.

After the failed attempt to pass me over to theology, they suggested I learn Polish as fast as I could. At least then that would qualify me to tap into primary-source material, and maybe then I could turn this around. Quickly, I realized that Polish is an unbelievably hard language to learn. In fact, it probably would have taken six to twelve years for me to learn Polish. Also, I realized this was a way for my department to stop me from writing any more inane material and instead put me in a sort of academic solitary confinement, where I would just go away and learn Polish. It would save everyone a lot of wasted hours of my writing and their reading my shitty papers.

Literally, the next reasonable step would be for them to buy back my tuition. Accepting that Holocaust studies was a dead end for me, I finished out the year, using a lethal combination of plagiarism and eating at Polish restaurants where I could order and hold brief conversations with waiters in Polish on the German killing operations in Poland (check out Podhalanka if you're in Chicago, and tell them the kid who talks about the Holocaust sent you).

With that, I give you a brief portion of my failed Holocaust memoir, in the great tradition of fake Holocaust memoirs (and fake memoirs of all kinds) of recent years, like those written by Misha Defonseca (who claimed she escaped the Warsaw ghetto and was raised by wolves), Binjamin Wilkomirski, Herman Rosenblat, et al. Many have tried to co-opt the monolithic tragedy that was the Holocaust for selfish purposes, and so, here, do I. Maybe it's the best way to exemplify another common human trait: "Those who can't do, lie." See if you spot some of the clues I've subtly placed that expose this as fake.

MY HOLOCAUST MEMOIR

CHAPTER 1

I remember less the way our modest half-timbered house looked but more the smell: pinewood, burnt leather, and choucroute. My father smoked a small briarwood pipe with a black mouthpiece and a smooth, almost pellucid chamber. When he kissed my cheek good night, his mustache was redolent with cherry pipe tobacco and kirsch.

When the Nazis came, I was seven. I heard a banging and then loud voices. I did what my mother had told me. I took my place underneath the large wooden dresser cabinet in the corner of my room. More loud voices. Then footsteps. Then, quiet. Cold, searing quiet.

I waited till dark to emerge. The front door was open and my father's pipe sat upright in the ashtray next to his armchair. I took a deep breath: pinewood, burnt leather, choucroute. From this point forward, everything had changed, and the spirits of the dead walked the earth. I remember myself when I was Jon Benjamin and I was seven and lived on 64 Rue Marbach. I even remember moments before, but that was someone else. Now, I was a phantom.

I walked out my front door and down the walkway, past the precise row of impatiens my mother had planted on Rue Marbach, and into the night filled with screams and the rumbling of motorcycle engines from some all-black bike gang that was roaming the night streets like in that movie *Biker Boyz*. Kid Rock was in that, and it was directed by Reggie Rock Bythewood.

I decided to be invisible and walked through Place Kléber, with the streetlamps burning reddish orange and groups of drunken revelers casting violent shadows across the cobblestones and onto the buildings that lined the square. Most Jews were being rounded up and sent to Drancy outside Paris, or so I was told. I kept walking, invisible, through the city streets, until the cobblestones turned to dirt and the dirt turned to pine thistle and mud and when I looked up, the densely leaved trees looked like sullen dizzy giants swaying in the night breeze. I fell asleep, hungry and cold, but overcome with a strange sense of calm, as if the forest itself was reading me a lullaby.

I dreamed of my mother laughing and father sitting in his chair as the teakettle whistled, and that scene in the movie *Biker Boyz* when Slick Will played by Eriq La Salle (yes, the guy who played Dr. Peter Benton from

ER) told the character Kid that when Smoke lines his bike up for a race, he doesn't see anything, he doesn't hear anything . . . just the finish line . . . Slick Will tells him, "Cat like that gets in the zone, it's like a gift from God," and then Kid stares right back at Slick Will and says, "Sounds like bullshit to me." Only minutes later, Slick Will was killed by an out-of-control bike that crashed into him during the end of a drag race.

Just seeing Eriq La Salle (spelled E-r-i-*q* . . . pretty ballsy, by the way, using a *q* in place of a *c* or *k*), really made me think about that other medical drama *St. Elsewhere* and that show's final episode, where they show the hospital and it is snowing, and they pull out to reveal that the hospital is in a snow globe, and the snow globe is being looked at by the autistic son of Dr. Westphall, but Dr. Westphall comes home and we see he's not even a doctor but a janitor or something who worked at St. Eligius Hospital, thereby concluding that the whole show had been the convoluted fantasy of an autistic child.

That's what it felt like that cold night in the forest in Neuhof, when the Nazis came to Alsace and the world became broken.

My Failed Book List

Your Kampf: Hitler's second book, about your struggle, not his.

1988: Orwell's follow-up about a synth-pop band called Thoughtcrime.

James Eyre: A novel about a dude getting laid all the time in the nineteenth century.

The Picture of Lori Ann Gray: The story of a woman who makes a very poor deal with the devil wherein she ages at the same rate as her portrait.

Waiting on Godot: A play about how tough it is being a server in a busy NYC restaurant.

The Most Oedipal Game: The story of an island where you can hunt and kill your father.

The Bird: A retelling of the Daphne du Maurier story *The Birds* (adapted into the famous Hitchcock movie) but with just one bird. One really crazy bird.

The Girls: An inversion of *The Birds* about a group of girls trying to kill a bird.

The Old Man and the TV: The story of an old man desperately trying to set up his Apple TV for more than four days, only to not be able to do it.

David Copperfeld: The story of a young man who one day becomes an accountant.

The Note: An old man reads from a Post-it to his lover who is afflicted with advanced Alzheimer's about where her pills are kept.

CHAPTER 12

Getting High
(and How I Failed at Being
Gay-Bashed)

I have always had a contentious relationship with marijuana. The first time I got high was at my friend Marc's house. Marc was my seventh-grade classmate and lived in an affluent neighborhood not far from where I lived. His house was sleek and modern and on a large meticulously landscaped property with varied and unique species of trees, like red ones and greenish ones and greenish-brown ones (I'm not an arborist), and a koi pond in the front. It was like visiting a Japanese temple.

His father was a businessman and usually sat in a leather chair with a large unlit cigar in his mouth reading a paper. He looked like he belonged there. He and the chair were in perfect union. The house was sprawling and, as a kid, the prospect of being able to wander into a separate wing with almost complete privacy was thrilling. It was the kind of house where it felt like Marc was more a lodger and less a family member, like a thirteen-year-old Kato Kaelin.

He had an older brother, who was a senior in high school and whose main and most memorable characteristic was that he dressed and acted like he was Southern. He wore jeans and a CSA belt buckle and drove a Trans Am with a confederate flag on it and a bale of hay in the back. It also had a Dixie horn. Look, the Confederacy was not well represented in New England in the early 1980s, so in this respect he was something of a vanguard figure. A bit controversial, but at the time, just another local kid with a very disturbing and comprehensive obsession with *The Dukes of Hazzard* whose parents, for some incomprehensible reason, bought him a tribute car to the Confederacy. Hey, at least it wasn't *Magnum, P.I.*, since Ferraris are way pricier. Despite his Confederate leanings, he was very sweet and, coincidentally, the first person to get me high.

It was in his room, country music was playing, and I was uncontrollably laughing for at least an hour. I also remember obsessing about getting an erection, and so I was laughing while forcefully pressing my hands into my crotch, holding back a phantom erection that I kept imagining I was getting. It must have appeared odd: me standing in a doorway giggling while jamming my penis and balls into my legs. As much fun as that first time was, I spent the next week with sore balls, and that would become a bellwether for my contentious relationship with pot that would continue until I stopped smoking, in my early forties. I guess one could make the argument that as much as I've tried, I am truly a failed pot smoker.

Almost every time I was saddled with some sort of intense anxiety or dissociative experience. But the drive to get this drug to be enjoyable for me was a real goal, seemingly unattainable, like my suburban version of summiting Everest. My brain chemistry and THC are just natural enemies, and in spite of all my efforts, smoking pot would inevitably leave me isolated, rocking back and forth and trying not to swallow my tongue.

In my early thirties, after a few months of dating, I decided to take my girlfriend Amy on our first trip together to Toronto. I had a friend who was from there, and he had arranged for his brother (who was a lifelong Toronto resident) to plan some stuff for us to do: tickets to a hockey game, etc. It was a very hockey-centric schedule, and that seemed good, considering Amy had no interest in hockey. I found that out during the hockey game and then after, at the Hockey Hall of Fame, or maybe at the bar after the game that showed exclusively hockey highlights.

The second night, we met my friend's brother for a beer at the Horseshoe Tavern, a famous music venue. After a bit, Amy was tired and went back to the hotel. My friend's brother and I stayed at the bar for a while and chatted about hockey. He said his friend was having a party in an apartment nearby, so we went. It was a walk-up apartment and very trap house–y: the party kind of sprawled out over various rooms, with people milling about, and in each room a different tableau of party tropes, like people doing coke on a table, and in another, a couple in flagrante delicto, and in another, a guy playing guitar and a girl on tambourine with a group of people gathered about (all right, not so trap house–y).

We went out onto a deck that overlooked the main street, and he lit a joint. I had the premonition, like every time I smoked pot, that I would lose my shit, but I took a hearty puff anyway, and within about seven seconds, I lost my shit.

It must be a curious thing to see me high, because in my estimation, I am like Schwarzenegger in *Total Recall* when his woman suit glitches out: "Two weeks, two weeks, twos weeeeeeeeeeeks . . ." and melts off. Luckily, this guy was a talker, and smoking pot compels more talking, so in this case (and most), I stood silently in a state of pure terror, while he made droll conversation.

As my mental state started to spiral and the party became a blur of light and sound, I made my way out knowing only that I had to get back to the hotel. Safety. Must go to safety. Must go to the hotel. The hotel I'm staying at. As I got to the street, there were like hundreds of people and hundreds of cars backed up, and that was not good for my state of mind. I was desperate to get back to my hotel, but I now couldn't remember the name of it or where it was, and my girlfriend had taken the key, so there was no hope of finding out.

I decided just to get a cab and then figure out what to do from there, like maybe ask the driver to list the names of all the hotels in Toronto so eventually I could hear it and remember. But it was actually impossible to get a cab. Someone in the crowd said to take the trolley, so I shakily made my way over to a trolley stop and sat there with a group of drunk women who were waiting as well. I sat like rigor mortis was setting in.

After what seemed like an hour, the women had peeled off, after a friend had miraculously gotten a cab. But I continued to sit, waiting for a trolley that would, in my mind, somehow take me to the hotel that I was staying at, without actually knowing where or what it was. I guess I just thought it may be a magic trolley, like the bus in *My Neighbor Totoro*.

Finally, a man approached, stirring me out of my mind spin and chirped with that clipped Canadian pitch, "No more trolleys." FUCK! FUCK! I was so fucked. I realized I had to go back to that house party to try to find my friend's brother just to avoid going to a hospital ER to sleep. But I was too high to find the house again, and now the bars were closed and the crowds were still thick in the streets and I couldn't think straight, so I summoned enough focus to hatch a plan.

I decided to try to retrace my path to the bar from the hotel by sight, based on the location of the CN Tower (an iconic very tall tower in Toronto). The one thing I knew was that the CN Tower was visible from the cab to the Horseshoe, so maybe I could find a path where the iconic and extremely tall CN Tower appeared in my vantage point the same way as when I saw it on the way, but in reverse. Follow?

I was convinced this theory would work, and somehow I would eventually land at the hotel whose name, still, I did not remember. But I figured I couldn't remember the name because I was high, and I knew that when I stopped being high, it would come back to me, but I also felt sure that I would never stop being high forever and ever. So I just started walking while looking up at the CN Tower, and when the tower was obscured by a building, I felt increasingly high and panicked and, in response, scurried to find the tower, like a terrified puppy. The CN Tower was now the center of the universe and my umbilical cord to a fragile sense of reality.

I must have walked some twenty minutes and the tower was a good ways off from where it had started in my eyeline so I felt like I was making progress. But this notion was quickly met with the stark realization that I was in the middle of nowhere, in some kind of barren warehouse area, and the streets were empty, save for the very occasional passing car. This brought me back to my natural state of pure panic, but I had my tower. That tireless, immoveable tower. My lighthouse. And then, a jolt from the dark. "Hey, faggot." I looked down and there were four teenagers. They were in a phalanx, and I was sort of relieved, but for the "Hey, faggot" part.

"Where you going, faggot?"

Okay, so he was sticking with the faggot thing, but there was still a glimmer of hope that they could help. Maybe, I thought, *faggot* was a familiar, friendly greeting in Toronto, like *mate* in Britain.

"To my hotel."

"To his hotel!"

A classic, familiar bit of repartee that signals bad things to come: when someone repeats what the other is saying in a slightly mocking fashion, a very common refrain signaling the beginning of hundreds and thousands of fights since the beginning of time.

"I'm lost, actually."

"The faggot is lost."

I only then started to realize that I was being gay-bashed. I pivoted to quickly provide insignificant details as an attempt to stall the inevitable.

"I can't find my hotel. I'm visiting here. I'm American."

"An American faggot."

I couldn't help laughing because of the way this kid said "an American faggot." It was actually poetic, with the combination of his thick Canadian accent and those choice and peculiar few words. It was like the title of a lost Walt Whitman poem. But my laugh struck the wrong chord for them.

"What are you laughing at, faggot?" Less Walt Whitman now. Then he pushed me hard, and I was like a rag doll anyway, but being that high, I just toppled over.

In these strange, heightened moments, the mind works

quickly, intuitively. I had been assessing the situation sub-consciously and I knew what I needed to do. This was a classic case of "appear weak when you are strong, and strong when you are weak." One swift blow to their leader, the loud one, the one who pushed me down and stood over me with a Cujo glower, and the others would cave and either scurry away or take me as their new leader. It was clear as Canadian Mist. Just as it is foretold and im-memorial. I would just quickly stand and punch him right in the neck, crushing his homophobic Adam's apple and choking his breath, leaving him helpless and buckled over in defeat.

Instead, as they gathered around in a fashion that was highly suggestive—me kneeling—I seized this pivotal moment and said, "Who wants to get blown by the faggot first?"

Let's be honest, I can't punch. A stillness cloaked the scene, like a cold calm before the rogue wave hits. The leader looked appalled. Like genuinely appalled. It was the invitation they had been waiting for, and now, they had their act of war.

I braced for my kick in the head, but instead came a blinding light and the sound of a loud horn blaring. The kids scattered and, directly in front of me, a car with its headlights on appeared. A woman stepped out, but I couldn't really see her in the lights, and then she just got back in the car and drove away, and I was left alone, shak-ing, less high from fear, and it immediately occurred to me. The Windsor Arms Hotel.

The next night, we met my friend's brother again for dinner, and this time he brought his other brother. Afterward, we were out front and he handed me a joint. Despite my better instincts, I took a small puff. It wouldn't be like that again. I only smoked a tiny amount. Seven seconds passed, and I went right back to losing my shit, then a desperate retreat to the Windsor Arms, where I decided to pace around the outside perimeter of the hotel over and over. I told Amy to stay in the entranceway so I knew she would be there. I walked around possibly thirty times, maybe more. Finally, close to dawn, I went up to the room to sleep it off. That's how you show a girl a good time in Canada.

Failed
Weed-Strain Reviews

Singapore Math

A hybrid strain, Singapore Math boasts a small, tightly wound bud that packs a huge punch—a real *high-ya!* Singapore Math produces an ultra-disciplined effect with strong cerebral overtones. It's a real left-side-of-the-brain experience, bringing on waves upon waves of logical rushes that cascade like a consistent system of equations. With hints of cherry and citrus, this high-performing buzz does carry with it some hard-core self-doubt and bouts of overpoliteness. Also, some have described stiffness in movement and manner, along with perma-smile. I highly recommend this strain if you like an intelligent, respectful stone with huge interior baggage and an abiding impulse to overwork. But I would avoid driving after smoking Singapore Math. It will aggravate other drivers.

Kentucky Coal

This S1 cultivar has royal origins—many believe it's the result of a cross between two of the same family of seeds, which gives Kentucky Coal its unusual appearance and powerfully dense attributes. Kentucky Coal is a workhorse that delivers a very introverted experience—some would say too introverted, as in cut off from normal society and its highfalutin' moral compass. Woodsy and dark, Kentucky Coal is long-lasting and stridently opinionated, bringing its smoker a creamy sanctimony followed by a radical sense of insularity. This is a great toke for just hanging out alone with your loved ones—or cousins or sister or uncle—and getting down and dirty.

Fratricide

There's nothing commonplace about this florid, richly green sativa-indica blend. It's all brawn and not much brain. Creative types need not apply, as this muscly buzz does not take no for an answer. On smoking Fratricide, a blanket sensation of entitlement washes over you, making this an ideal bud to share with buds who are also of the mind-set that no consequence is too damaging. It's a real team-effort high. One downside to this musky blend is the aftermath, which can be a bit prickly. But don't worry—your parents and/or a white judge will probably bail you out.

Daddy Issues

Sharp and unforgiving, this bitter bud is the hard pillow on the bed, the one you try to avoid but somehow end up sleeping on. This is hard smoke to swallow, and it leaves a deep feeling of regret and existential dread with a lingering premonition that things will just get worse. The high then morphs into a growing parental anxiety about future un-fulfilled burdens. Finally, Daddy Issues snowballs into a revolving sense of the cycles of eternity, of knowing that your life is connected to all life before it and all life that follows and that you've only contributed to that and that alone—which ends up being a devastating truth. (By the way: Don't smoke this Pandora's box too late at night; you've got to take your kid to school in the morning.)

Tween Green

Middle school can be a high-pressure environment. You've got to dutifully perform at school, stay connected socially, feel vulnerable all the time, and then go home and get shit for all that. These trying years can have lasting effects, and this strain is the perfect antidote for them. So I'm not advocating tween smoking, but I am advocating Tween Green for those people stuck in their memories of the many horrible experiences middle school can bring. This is a nice, smoothed-out ride with intermittent flashes of the distant memory of a kid calling you "fat fuck," or an-other kid dumping out a saltshaker on your head in the cafeteria because you like disco (callback), or you having your period all over your beige pants in the middle of so-cial studies.

Kosher Kush

Next year in Jah-rusalem! Sometimes, the rigors of the modern high are too much to take. Sometimes we crave a simpler high, one that forgoes the imposing freedoms of the infinite permutations a typical high can bring. Sometimes we just want a radically narrow high, what some would call a *purposeful* high. The double K offers this with a vengeance. But don't sell your donkey before you build your cart; the double K comes with a lot of baggage. Maybe it's better explained sermonically. There's an old story, oft told, about a farmer who lived in a small hut with his wife and his baby. For months and months, no rain came and the farmer was hard-pressed to grow the crops necessary to sustain him and his family. Every day he would sit in his field and pray to God for rain to nourish the soil to grow the crops. Then one day the wife came with her baby to the man who sat in his arid field and she showed him the baby's penis, which was red and irritated on the tip. She was worried that the baby was carrying disease. Suddenly, as from nowhere, a torrential rain came. The farmer was overjoyed. And it rained and rained. For weeks, the rains came and the farmer sat in his hut waiting for it to stop, but it never did. What he assumed was a gift became a curse, for his fields flooded and he could still not grow any crops. He then knew that the baby's red penis was a very convoluted test from God to make things that appear good actually bad. Now, to this day, the Jewish people cut the tips off their babies' penises and do very little farming. Kosher Kush can be a bit like this test, so best be careful not to apply too much significance to what you smoke, or you may get stuck in your ways—and that ends up hurting babies.

CHAPTER 13

How I Failed to Sell a Pilot

I spent my twenties pretty much getting fired from a bunch of waitering jobs but did finally land a steady gig stacking books at the Cambridge Public Library in Cambridge, Massachusetts. It was a pretty good job, if you enjoyed public masturbation and cleaning up after public masturbation. It was also good if you like to get paid less than thirteen thousand a year. I spent a lot of my nights then trying to do comedy at places like Catch a Rising Star and Stitches Comedy Club with various sketch troupes. Years went by, and I still can't honestly say that I had any real ambition to do comedy as a profession. The comedians around me, who performed night in and night out, their aim was pretty apparent—become successful at comedy. At first, I thought of comedy as a way to avoid a profession, but via all these people I was around, very driven comedy minds, I learned to mimic their drive to pursue comedy as an actual career. But that doesn't go without error.

Having been a part of many sketch shows and appearing in a couple of animated shows, I started to slowly develop a comedy-writing career. Pitching and writing shows is a precarious endeavor. I have written a good number of sitcom scripts with the hopes that they'll get developed into series. But writing television pilots can become a tedious task, because often, you have a good idea for a show, it gets sold, and then you spend time and energy writing it and then the network takes months to get back to you and their notes come in and they want to make changes and the process becomes entangled and unclear. By this time, you are so far away from the moment of conception that the idea itself starts to seem terrible and fruitless, so you end up rooting for its demise. It's like any relationship really.

My first script for a network was called *Squash Club*. It was 1996, and I had just moved to New York and was, for some reason, playing a lot of squash at a club downtown. I didn't really have a day job, so it was a good time to score open court. The script, appropriately, was about a young man who played squash with old men in New York City and they became his only friends. It was really about not wanting to be young—something I strongly felt in real life. Being young means you have so much left to do, but being old means just settling in quietly for the remaining days. You know, just tucking yourself in with a bowl of popcorn or some soup and welcoming the final breath (that's how I imagine my death—being poisoned by soup).

Anyway, the pilot script was declined, and I moved

on to the next idea, which was subsequently rejected, and so on, for many, many years. Also, there's this sword of Damocles–type feeling about starting the process, and it's twofold, because one, once you start, you're almost certain it will reap no reward and die on the vine; and two, if the show does get picked up, but the idea was concocted more out of necessity than inspiration, it's less than ideal knowing you have to helm a show you just came up with as an exercise in coming up with something for the sake of coming up with something.

Oh, and for money. It turns out writing pilots is a pretty low-paying affair considering the amount of time invested, most of which is waiting for a response. Basically, writing pilots for television has a very low rate of return emotionally and financially. That's some uplifting advice for all you young writers getting into television.

I am the king of gloomy feedback. Around the same time as the writing of *Squash Club*, I remember going once to a high school as a volunteer to an enrichment program for kids, where I met with several classes to talk about animation and scriptwriting. After the classes ended, there was a final ceremony in the school's auditorium, where the volunteers sat on stage and went down the line giving their final thoughts to the students. All successful artists and actors and musicians, all so incredibly positive. Like "Never stop striving and working toward your dreams," and "Don't let anything stand in the way of going for it."

An actor, I think it was Matthew Lillard, spoke right

before me, and he was fired up. He gave this rousing speech about achieving goals by pushing to be who you want to be. It hit all the major notes, and undeniably was a bit of hokum, but it was well-delivered and incredibly well-received hokum. Kids like positive reinforcement.

I resented his success and his positive reinforcement, and then it was my turn. I went for some irony and told the kids, as a counterpoint, not to push so hard, because "going for it" is annoying. So many blank stares. Even my fellow volunteers on stage, none of whom I knew, looked at me sideways. It was a poorly timed joke.

You never know when a joke is going to fall completely flat. I have had many jokes in this vein produce rotten results. One that springs to mind was when, during the era of answering machines, I recorded my and my girl-friend Amy's outgoing message so it said, "Hi, you've reached Jon and Amy, we're not here right now, but if you need to reach us, please call [the number of the White House]." Not a great joke, but when Amy's grandmother tried to reach her, she called the White House and started leaving messages for someone there who actually shared Amy's name. In the end, I made an old woman very confused and disappointed that her granddaughter was not working for President Clinton.

Back in the late nineties, my friend and I sold a pilot to NBC. The show's premise was pretty simple. It was about two twentysomething guys who were going nowhere fi-nancially, so they decide to just "retire" and move into one of their grandparents' gated community in Florida to save money and scam old people. I can't remember the title, but I imagine it was something like, *Early Retirement* or *Gated* or *Buddies* or *Moving In* or *Hi, Grandma, I'm Home* or *And Bubbie Makes Three* or *It Takes a Retirement Village.*

When we started writing, I suggested that we might take a bit of the money we were going to make and go to Florida, where my brother-in-law's parents lived, and spend a night at their Jewish retirement village to do some embedded research for the script. They lived in Boca Raton, the Babylon of Jewish retirement: an endless stream of golf course condominium communities separated by strip malls. Now, I'm not exactly very close with my brother-in-law's father and mother, but they were gracious enough to agree to show us around their community. When we arrived, we told them we just wanted to tag along with them as they did what they would normally do so we could get a sense of the lifestyle.

It was pretty much what you would imagine. A trip to the clubhouse and the pool for lunch, then a trip to a nearby strip mall, to some weird gambling facility that kinda looked illegal—all the windows were blacked out, but inside there were just slot machines. After that, the requisite 5:00 p.m. discount buffet dinner at an all-you-can-eat Chinese food place. At the dinner, crammed into a booth, the father told us how he was his community's head writer for his theater group that put on in-house plays and performances, and went into a detailed description of his body of work, which consisted mainly of Jewish parody versions of postwar musicals. So, for example, the

Jewish *West Side Story* (*West Side Schnorrer*), or the Jewish *Cats* (*Katz*), or the Jewish *My Fair Lady* (*My Fair Knaidel*). A simple refillable model for quick-impact entertainment for old Jews. Basically any Yiddish pun would suffice. That's a special talent, writing stuff like that.

I pulled my cowriter aside and hit him with what I thought was an interesting proposal. We could take a decent but minority-share percentage out of our paycheck for the script and have my brother-in-law's father write the whole thing and then turn that in to the studio just to see what happens. Again, in my spirited tradition, a way for me to make less money than I could, but in this case, the same for my cowriter, who was not as thrilled with the idea. I convinced him next to the heaping glossy load of chicken and broccoli under a sneeze guard, and we went back to our table to offer our new writer the opportunity. He was thrilled.

So, now, to summarize, we were paying something around $4,000 out of what I think was about $20,000 total to a retired shoe salesman we only knew peripherally to write a whole sitcom script for us to turn in in lieu of something written by us . . . as a joke . . . or not? And let's be clear, money was an issue for us, and giving away 20 percent off the top also factors in to the normal deductions one takes in this line of work, where we also have to pay off our agent, our manager, and our taxes. So, this joke would cost us 20 percent more than the 50 percent taken out of our payment. We would end up with around

$2,500 for the script each, minus the money we were paying to go to Boca for research, which was also my idea.

So most would say this was a lark. But maybe his script would be good and he'd become the next septuagenarian head writer of a network sitcom. I'm saying, in these kinds of experiments, there is no set conclusion, though one would guess it would not work out well for any of us. But like I've been trying to tell you, this is my unique talent: to successfully muck up any plan. It stems from a complex that manifests as my taking pleasure in hurting myself and others simultaneously, a real Freudian one-man band.

Back in New York, around three weeks later, we received a script about forty pages long with little to no connection to our story and with an extremely disproportionate amount of Viagra jokes. It wasn't at all what the network would want but exactly what we wanted for the network. At least, for the reaction.

Also, I will point out, this was in no way a failure on the part of the father-in-law. He wrote a whole sitcom script in three weeks with no real television experience—despite, I gather, a heavy reliance on Jewish joke books, which could be construed as plagiarism, but I am not here to judge his methods. I'm here to make people uncomfortable. Also, if no action had been taken in that Chinese buffet that night in Boca Raton, I would not have this to share with you. Here is a snippet from the pilot script written by my brother-in-law's father, Mal.

Man 1: Ernie's wife asked him if he remembered if they ever had a mutual orgasm. He answered, "No, we always had State Farm." (*All laugh.*)

Man 2: Hey, what do you get when you mix Viagra with your baked beans for supper?

All: What d'ya get?

Man 2: A stiff wind. (*Everyone laughs.*)

Man 1: There was a truckload of Viagra hijacked last night. The police were told to be on the lookout for a gang of hardened criminals.

Man 2: How about the old guy in the nursing home. They gave him Viagra every night to keep him from falling out of bed.

Man 1: Did you hear the one about the old geezer who said to his doctor, "I think I'm going deaf in my right ear"? The doctor said, "No wonder you can't hear, you have a suppository stuck in there." The old geezer said, "Now I know what happened to my hearing aid!"

Now, I like a good Viagra joke (actually, not really), but three hundred in a row gets to be a little much. And the script was magnificently outdated, but to be fair, perfectly outdated. George Eliot and Raymond Chandler didn't write until later in their lives, and think how much better *Middlemarch* would have been with more (any) Jewish jokes. Or erectile dysfunction jokes. But this was definitively not a modern American sitcom. It was more like Soviet psyops.

So, the plan unfolded. We sent his script as ours and waited. About three weeks later, we got on the phone with the executives from NBC to discuss the draft and had a gloriously uncomfortable notes call. They tried as best they could to politely explain that the script seemed to be "trying too hard to capture the characters of a Florida old-age community." They were expecting something more from the perspective of the young characters and felt there were way too many old-timey Jewish jokes. But they did break it down and give suggestions on how to retool it in great depth. At the end of the call, we revealed what we did, and there was a pregnant pause. Like more of a baffled "Why would you do this?" than a "That's an amusing gag." We did make them read and pull together a half hour of notes on a script we didn't write.

Anyway, I thought it was funny, and they ended up passing on our deal. A win-win in my book. And a win for my brother-in-law's father. But a loss for my writing partner, who I still feel I owe money to for souring any prospects with that network for some time. But we will always have that one night in Boca, when hope was alive and we were young and they were old and money meant nothing (to me) and Chinese food was $3.99.

As a quick addendum, in keeping slightly on message, I'd like to offer a side story in the spirit of confused grandmothers and Jewish jokes. Maybe my reputation for unfortunate phone pranking precedes me, or maybe it was just an unusual coincidence.

When my grandmother Sadie was alive, I would frequently speak to her. At least once a week. She lived alone in the Bronx after my grandfather passed away. She was an incredible woman. Small, sturdy, almost indestructible. Even in her nineties, she lugged groceries up the steep hill to her apartment complex.

One day, she called me and asked me if I was feeling better. I said, "Why do you ask?"

"Because you were so sick the last time you called, Jonny."

"Grandma, I haven't been sick in over a year."

"Well, you certainly sounded it," she explained.

"Why?" I asked.

"Because you sounded all stuffed up and asked me if I was alone and what I was wearing, and when I told you I was in my housecoat, you started to breathe heavily, and I kept saying, 'Jonny, are you all right?' But you kept breathing heavily, then moaned and hung up."

"That wasn't me, Grandma."

"Then who else could it have been?"

CHAPTER 14

Prince Edward Island (and How I Failed to Take a Walk in the Woods)

As I previously mentioned, when I was twelve, my parents sent me to that 4-H camp, mainly because my friend was going and his family had horses on their small farm in Westborough, Massachusetts, making him a horse guy and someone who actually wanted to go to horse camp. I, on the other hand, was allergic to every land animal imaginable. I couldn't even have a hamster in my house or I would break into hives.

My mother also had a phobia of dogs. Whenever a dog came near she would turn into a statue, unable to talk. This would make for interesting scenarios when neighbors would come by, walking their dogs. It was always a one-way conversation.

Neighbor: Hello, Shirley!
My mom: (*Frozen glare.*)
Neighbor: How's Howie doing?
My mom: (*Frozen glare.*)
Neighbor: Ummm, hi, Jon.
Me: Hi.
Neighbor: Well, nice to see you, Shirley.
My mom: (*Frozen glare.*)
Neighbor: (*Muttering.*) Jesus, what a fucking jerk.

Eventually, the dog owners in my neighborhood became aware of her phobia and learned my mother wasn't some monumental asshole or some KGB agent who spoke no English sent to destroy America. Anyway, as you can glean, animals were not our thing.

Horse camp? I was dreading it. I knew it would be a week of me wheezing and missing my phobic mommy. But imagine, to learn how to ride a horse! That's the stuff of warriors and princes (and peasants and serfs). The camp was about a forty-minute drive from my house, and I got dropped off with my duffel bag and met up with my horse friend. At the time, he was really into girls and he immediately starting rating them during the introduction meeting in the main cabin, as all the campers were gathered.

For him, this was the pinnacle of excitement. An overnight camp with horses and girls. For me, this was a nightmare. An overnight camp with horses and girls. I bristled at the thought of meeting girls, with labored, allergic breathing, even though there's nothing sexier than a good hearty wheeze to impress a woman. The first task was to head to the stables to meet the horses and get a basic sense of what the daily regimen would be. Wheezing ensued as the counselors introduced us to all the horses that I would hate riding for the next week. After, we went to the main hall to have dinner. With a semi-obstructed airway, I tried to get my food down. I knew I would spend my time at this camp exclusively with the camp nurse.

Then, suddenly, out of nowhere, there was a muffled scream, then from across the room, a girl, maybe about thirteen years old, stumbled from the bathroom, her hands held up over her head with blood running down her arms. Counselors escorted her out quickly. We all just sat there in silence. No one knew what was going on. For a long time, we sat, until an ambulance arrived, the flickering red lights filling the room. Finally, the camp director came in and announced that a girl had cut her wrists in the bathroom in a suicide attempt. It was a bit stunning that he didn't at least play it down a bit. Horse people don't mince words.

He invited any camper to call their parents to pick them up in the event they did not want to continue based on what had happened. My friend sat there stunned. A few kids got up and headed for the door. I looked at my friend, took a shallow breath that made a high-pitched *heeeeeee* sound, and got up to leave. I drove home with this strange feeling of relief, shaded by the tragic circumstance of a girl, who, out of nowhere, at some remote 4-H camp, cut both her wrists.

Maybe she hated the thought of going to horse camp more than me, or maybe she was just troubled, but either way, her actions set me free. I hope she is okay, but to this day whenever I see a horse, I think of that girl.

When I was in my late thirties, I wanted to take a trip with Amy before we had our baby. She was about six months pregnant, and we both felt we needed one last fling with freedom before we were saddled with the excruciating pleasure of raising a child. She wanted to go to Mexico, to the beach. I had never been. I was slightly uncomfortable with the idea of Mexico. I was sure it was great, but I have an aversion to "great." Everyone I know had been to Mexico and enjoyed it, therefore "Why go?" It's like a compulsion to reject norms. My feeling is why go to a luxury resort, when you could go to rural Minnesota and tour a packing house or to Peaks Island, Maine, to go to the Umbrella Cover Museum?

It was almost winter, so naturally I suggested the most inopportune place: Nova Scotia. "Are you sure you want to go to Nova Scotia off-season, when Mexico would be perfect?" she said.

"It'll be more interesting," I answered.

We flew to Halifax and stayed at a small B & B situated on a promontory overlooking a quiet harbor. It was one of those bed-and-breakfasts where people are friendly and everyone eats breakfast together. Because neither of us is friendly, this was extremely awkward. The next day we decided to leave Nova Scotia altogether and take the ferry to Prince Edward Island, an even more remote province.

The ferry to the island was enormous, and there were only about four people on it. And when we docked, things looked pretty barren. A guy with a Billy Gibbons beard sat behind a picnic table selling wooden clocks shaped like Prince Edward Island itself. You couldn't even get a bottle of water, but you could buy a homemade clock from a Canadian hillbilly. (No offense, hillbillies.)

We figured we would head to town and grab lunch before we went to our inn. There were two things open: a fish restaurant and a knife factory. We ate at the fish restaurant, which was empty. The waitress told us it was off-season. Things pick up again in May, she said. After lunch, we strolled over to the knife factory and bought a bread knife. Then we went to our inn, which, like everywhere else we had been on this trip, was located on a quaint harbor. (No offense, quaint harbors.)

The next morning, we planned to head to a national forest and take a walk. We're not very outdoorsy, but there wasn't much else to do unless we wanted to get daywork at a sawmill. We filled a backpack and headed in the car to the other side of the island, intent on embracing our isolation. It might not be fun, but we would give ourselves over to the solitude of nature.

We pulled up and looked at the wooden placard that marked the trails. A huge expanse of forest unfolded before us. We chose the one-and-a-half-mile loop. I mean, we wanted outdoor adventure, but a very small amount. We zipped up our jackets and plunged into the deep Canadian wilderness.

As we made our way, the forest grew quiet, and trees canopied us from the light. We walked through in silence. About fifteen minutes in, we were doing relatively well, although I could sense a mild level of dread. There was a definite forced peacefulness, like a grimace and a teeth-clenched "Isn't this a nice walk?" As we turned a corner, I saw it, only a few yards in front of us, looming in the center of the path. A sizable brown clump. A whopping pile of animal dung. And this was not some ordinary pile. A massive load. We approached it slowly. It was still steaming.

"This looks like fresh bear shit," I said.

I saw her face go ashen. Diplomatic, I repeated, "This is definitely bear shit." (Note: I have no idea what bear shit looks like.) Somehow I'd forgotten then that bears attack people and that this might alarm her, who, remember, had a baby in her, but more to the point, I was distracted by my mortal terror that a bear was near. Her look turned to horror, and our peaceful walk suddenly shifted in tone.

She started striding ahead down the path, murmuring incoherently. Her fear exacerbated my fear, and I ran ahead, senselessly babbling out ideas of what we should do if confronted by a bear. She quickened to keep up with me, taking heavy breaths and exhaling loudly and rhythmically. We looked like we were in a speed-walk race. She sounded as if she were in labor. I eventually stopped talking, and we walked together at this clipped pace, staring straight ahead in a full state of panic.

Everything went away except the primal instinct to survive. The last thing I remember saying was: "Don't run. Just walk fast."

Suddenly, I heard something coming from behind us. I didn't even want to turn around. I was certain this was it. Who would the bear take first? Would I sacrifice myself to save my girlfriend and our baby? The sound grew louder. Instantly and without fanfare, two teenage girls in jogging shorts swept past us in a split second. They smiled and waved hello. My girlfriend and I looked at each other blankly. We walked the rest of the path and back to the car.

Amy wanted to leave the next day, a day earlier than we planned. I could only comply. On our way home, I bought a wooden clock from the hillbilly as a keepsake of our island journey. When I look back on that trip, I wonder why I wanted it to be that bad. Maybe when you set your sights very low, you can't be overly disappointed. But we will always have that shared experience of sort of possibly being potentially attacked by a bear. That stands out more than some great trip to some eco-resort in Cozumel. Plus, I still have that bread knife.

CHAPTER 15

How I Failed as a New Father

The moment when I decided to ejaculate I knew that there was a possibility of future fatherhood. But I was playing the odds. I think it was not the best gamble: an inverted Russian roulette, if you will. Anyway, it was a boy, and I cried when I found out. I was at the O'Hare airport when Amy told me by phone. That's why we named him Sbarro. I admit I was, at best, confused by the notion that I was to be a parent, but comforted by the fact that millions had done poorly before me.

Our son was delivered by C-section, and my first thought as I entered the OR was *Why do they not have an entrance where you don't have to walk by the disemboweled body of your partner before crossing past the partition?* I know people record their births, but there is a reason nobody records their C-sections. Amy, with the help of much medication, seemed unaware that her insides were draped like dirty laundry on her chest, which is a good thing I suppose.

When my baby was shown to me by the doctor moments later, my mood was already ruined by the sight of internal organs. My girlfriend kept complaining she was cold, and I imagine it was because her entire lower half was splayed open. Anyway, I don't want to grouse too much, but just a quick revamping of the entryway would have really changed my first-time-father moment. From there, it went downhill.

First misstep: I did not spend the first night in the hospital with my girlfriend. The baby is kept in a nursery separated except for feedings, so I figured I would go out to dinner. Oh, and it wasn't purely selfish (the dinner part), since I was going home to pick up fresh clothes for her, but it was worth getting admonished by the bartender as I ordered a glass of red wine.

"I just had a baby."

"Congratulations, when?"

"About four hours ago."

A sour look crossed his face. "Oh, well, what are you doing here?"

He didn't seemed pleased with my "getting some clothes at home" answer and peered at me as I sat masticating roast duck. I was like Henry I, checking quickly on "just another male heir" and then back to the banquet. I have fond memories of that duck, though.

Second miscalculation: when driving your partner home from the hospital with your baby in a used car in midwinter with poor heating, don't say, "I need to stop at

Duane Reade to pick up my medication." Also, after she says no, don't argue that it's on the way. And don't stop. But I did. I have high cholesterol. It was being treated with medication. It was pretty much on the way home.

I will say that I was highly underprepared to be a father. It is difficult for a narcissist to focus his attention elsewhere, and so I didn't. During the first few months, I did spend a lot of time with my son. And I know from research that in those early days, it is important to provide reassurance, so our days were mainly spent at a newly opened video game bar in the East Village, reassuring me.

This childcare haven was generally empty until the neighborhood schools got out at three thirty, so I would have a good five hours of playing system link *Halo* with my baby watching. It takes a village to save Earth from the Covenant. I neglected to tell my girlfriend that our newborn was primarily being reared indoors to the sounds of assault rifles. But look, that sound is not far off from the echoed sounds of a mother's beating heart, so I was mainly providing aural consistency.

Third misstep: The park, in NYC, is basically a second home for child-rearing. A good part of early childhood is spent in parks. And a community forms among those who populate the parks. It's where moms and dads and their children form early bonds. It is also where early petty resentments develop. The park is a breeding ground for parents to judge other parents and develop private animosities toward them, the caregivers, and the children.

The first and easiest target, for me, was the toddler with the electric-powered car (at least it wasn't diesel), driving around recklessly wearing the Ed Hardy onesie and sunglasses. Sunglasses on toddlers are wrong. Adult accoutrements on babies are wrong. The act of even partially dressing toddlers as adults is creepy, unless you are dressing them as your favorite occupation, like a chef or an airline pilot or a coal miner. I think it would be refreshing to see a baby dressed in coveralls with soot on his face.

But this kid was just an attention seeker. Toddler douchebags are a puzzling group, mainly because they don't know they are douchebags yet, which just outwardly fuels their douchebaginess. It's an interesting conundrum, because adult douchebags are also mostly clueless about being douchebags, and that's in essence what makes them douchebags. They think their loud boorishness and ostentation is just a sign of confidence and good spirit. But the smug look on the face of the kid who gets put into an electric-powered mini Hummer may just as easily be the confounded face of a toddler, not necessarily the look of someone who is prodigiously indifferent to the poor.

But it is more likely an indicator of early-onset douchebag. I mean, how could you ever not end up cravenly wanting more, when, at five, you're already driving an electric Hummer?

The park is also a forum for public judgment on how children are raised, and many are not shy about sharing opinions. I wasn't immune to this. I mean, I judged a five-year-old just for driving a toy car. I judged parents for being overly precious about their babies. I judged parents who spoke harshly to other people's children. I pushed theories of parenting that I knew very little about. In the case of the Scandinavian couple who left their child in a stroller outside a bar in New York City while they went in to drink and defended it as a cultural norm in Scandinavia, I openly supported the couple, because of my wanting to do that here in America.

So, imagine how others judged me. One afternoon, I had brought my baby son to the park near our apartment. He had just started to crawl, so this was a huge uptick in excitement for our time together. Prior to this, there was the watching my baby lie and the watching my baby eat. Now, with this new skill, there was the watching my baby crawl. It's not a huge thing, but weeks and weeks go by where very little happens, so even slight changes make a big difference in the day to day. I took him out of the stroller to let him crawl freely and got myself in a sturdy position to watch.

Soon, I struck up a conversation with a young mother who was there with her own baby. After a few moments, another woman approached and asked, "Is that your baby?" She pointed to my baby, who was sitting next to a tree, perched up, moving his mouth in a chewing motion.

"Yes," I said.

"He's eating dog shit," she said.

I looked over and, yes, there was a dark brown material in his mouth. So many emotions flowed. I ran over and discovered that, yes, the dark brown material he was eating was the aforementioned dog shit, or maybe human shit, but definitely shit. So this was the moment when my baby was eating shit.

I used my finger to clear it out, but there was no determining how much had been eaten. Time was blurry at this point. Could it have been a whole log? Is more shit worse than a little shit? What is the protocol for baby shit-eating? Is it considered healthy in some cultures? Like do ashrams practice shit-eating as a way to develop stomach flora? Sweaty and panicked, I looked over to see the two women looking at me, both like, "How could you let your baby eat shit?"

I was in a full-blown panic, so I couldn't help thinking of myself, even as I cleared the remaining crap out of my son's mouth. My son was smiling, almost knowingly smiling, like "What are you going to do now?" I quickly asked the two mothers who were silently judging me if they knew whether it was imperative that I take him to the ER. Simultaneously, I thought of the repercussions, like "How do I even admit to the attending nurse that I let my son eat shit?" I know I should have been thinking of him first, and I know it seems simple enough, but pride is a powerful emotion. And it was early on in the process, so admitting to a failure this catastrophic was a really bad look.

In simple terms, was there a way, just . . . wondering . . . if this matter could go away? Like, could I get some water and wash him clean and we hope for the best, or do we have to go through the whole my-telling-everyone-my-baby-ate-shit thing? Hoping for some direction, I turned to the two women who had witnessed the incident. One immediately said, "I would take him to the ER," and the other quickly followed with, "I wouldn't worry about it." This was the absolute worst possible outcome: a split decision. I really needed clarity, but they argued back and forth while I listened on.

In an effort to protect myself and my growing reputation as a father, I chose the path of least resistance: hoping for the best. I went home and flushed out his mouth off and on for about two hours and then dressed him in his mother's favorite outfit. That evening, when Amy got home, she asked how the day was and I told her, just another day at the park. We looked over at our son, who sat in his bouncy chair pushing himself up and down with his baby legs, wearing a real shit-eating grin.

I will say that, in my case, doing nothing worked out, but I would not offer that claim as a general rule for any time a baby eats shit.

CHAPTER 16

How I Failed at Providing Some Historical Perspective on Failure Redux

W hen putting my failures into context, one has to consider the environment I come from. And not just my family and my heritage, but the actual place where I am from. With that, we can pin some blame on the failures of early America and see how those failures gave root to our personal failures. Maybe if I could learn a bit about why America's manifest success is not what it seems, I could better understand my failures as a product thereof. Most Americans, at this point in our history, feel like America is essentially a success story, but one has to look deeper in order to get a sense of the cracks that developed from its early settlement. I reached out to Temple University Native American history professor Andrew Isenberg to bring some clarity to this matter and to better lay out how certain aspects of America's culture were doomed to fail from the beginnings of our journey as a nation based on failures of communication and basic misunderstandings. Here is a transcript of the exchange.

May 17, 2017 10:52 AM

Professor Isenberg,

My name is Jon Benjamin, and I'm writing a book having to do with my personal failures in my life and I just checked my word count and my publishing contract obligates me to write over seventy-five thousand words, and I'm not even halfway there and my deadline is in two weeks, so pardon me, but I'm fucked. I know this seems out of the blue, but is there any way you can write a little bit about how the colonists failed with the Indians for me? It would be a real help, word count wise. I tried with another professor earlier in my writing process and he stopped writing me back. Hopefully, you can see it in your heart to help me. If not for anything else, to get your very important work out there to be seen by more people.

Jon

May 19, 2017 6:43 PM

I'm sorry about your predicament. Your
question is quite broad. In any survey of
encounters between settlers and Indians, one
doesn't have to look too hard to find "failures."
At the same time, as a historian, I don't go
looking for failures, or successes. I'm just trying
to figure out what happened and why.

Maybe the most important failure, at least
during the first encounters between colonists
and Indians, was the failure of both sides to
understand each other. Columbus called the
native inhabitants of the Americas "Indians"
because he thought he was in the Indies.
Spanish conquistadors in Mexico referred to
the temples in Tenochtitlan as "mosques"
because they reminded them of the mosques the
Moors had worshipped in in Spain, before they
had driven them out. The English settlers in
Massachusetts at first didn't believe that the
Indians' agricultural plots were real farms,
because the Indians didn't plant in neat rows
but rather put the corn, beans, and squash
together in one field (so that the bean plants
could climb up the cornstalks, while the squash
spread out on the ground). The English thought
these plants were just growing wildly.

More failures to understand: When European colonists showed up in the Americas, they accidentally brought with them the microbes that cause smallpox and measles. These diseases were previously unknown in the Americas, so no Indians had any acquired immunities. When the diseases first struck Indian communities, many of them did precisely the wrong thing— rather than quarantine those who were suffering, everyone would gather around them to help them, which only allowed the microbe to spread more easily. It's not that colonists understood what was happening much better. Most adult colonists had been exposed to these diseases as children in Europe and survived, and thus had acquired lifelong immunities. But both Catholic and Protestant religious leaders attributed the deaths of the Indians and the health of the colonists to divine providence. John Winthrop, the first governor of Massachusetts, wrote in 1634 that "the natives, they are all nere dead of the small Poxe, so as the Lord had cleared our title to what we possess."

Indians and colonists at first failed to understand each other when they signed agreements over land. It is not true that Indians had no conception of land ownership. They had a clear sense of usufruct rights—the rights to use property without owning it. Usufruct rights could be exclusive: in other words, we can hunt here but you can't. When some of the first treaties were signed between Indians and Europeans, the Indians thought they were granting the colonists the shared use of the land; they thought they were granting usufruct rights to the colonists. They were rather surprised to find out that the colonists thought they were acquiring the land outright. Also, the Indians assumed the colonists were going to live under their jurisdiction. When Chinese investors buy a condo in one of Jared Kushner's buildings, the condo does not become part of China. But when the colonists purchased lands from the Indians, they assumed that they had removed that land from the legal jurisdiction of the Indians who had sold it. The Indians did not necessarily assume the same thing—they were permitting the English to live in their territory under their jurisdiction. But the Europeans' belief that they were sovereign is what made them colonists rather than immigrants.

May 19, 2017

Professor Isenberg,

Jesus! That is really good and interesting. Wow, the other guy didn't do half as much and wouldn't when asked. He actually just gave me a list of resource materials and told me to do it. It seems like you could write a whole book.

May 20, 2017

Jon,

Actually I have written a few books, most of which have traveled under the radar except in some small academic circles.

Drew

May 20, 2017

Professor,

What are the books?

Jon

May 21, 2017

Jon,

One was called *The Destruction of the Bison*, another called *Mining California*, and a third called *Wyatt Earp: A Vigilante Life*. Some people didn't like that one because they thought I was saying that Wyatt Earp was gay.

Drew

May 21, 2017

Wait, Wyatt Earp was gay??!!!

Jon

May 23, 2017

Jon,

He shared a bed with another guy. For a year. But the book was mainly about his life and the politics of the time in that region of the country.

Drew

May 23, 2017

Andrew,

That certainly sounds gay, but it is hard to tell. There were fewer beds back then? I have a quick idea. Would you like to republish your book as my book? It would take a lot of pressure off me to continue writing and, at minimum, I would know an interesting well-researched book was out there under my name. It would also get your work out there to a bigger audience, as I mentioned previously. I know it's a lot to ask, but just think about it. I think I could at least reuse a portion of your material to cover the remainder of my required word count. I'm sure you know how hard it is to write a whole book, since you've done three. Anyway, think about it. Maybe we could eventually make a movie about a gay Wyatt Earp. That would be huge, like *Brokeback Mountain* meets Wyatt Earp?

Jon

May 24, 2017

Jon,

I don't think that would work legally with my publisher, plus wouldn't it be odd to just switch the topic of your book midway through? I think that might confuse your readers. I appreciate your interest in history, but I don't think this will work logistically. Good luck with your project.

Drew

Andrew,

Okay, I get it, but what if we publish a bunch of copies of your book with my cover on it, seeing my book is called *Failure Is an Option* and the stories are predominately about my failures, but in the case of those copies that have your book in place of mine, the "failure" is on the buyer to get my actual book. Pretty clever right?

Jon

Jon,

I'm not clear on why you would do anything like this.*

Drew

* I almost convinced my publisher to do this, but in the end they said no. A failure of a failure.

CHAPTER 17

How I Failed at
"the Celebrity Favor"

I know many people who are known for their work as actors, musicians, and comedians. For instance, I know Aziz Ansari. I also know Josh Groban. (Actually, I don't. But I'm sure if I did, he would be pleasant enough.) I once was photographed by paparazzi standing next to Sarah Jessica Parker at a street corner and it was published in *Us Weekly* and I lied to everybody that I was friends with her.

One of the perks of being a celebrity or a public figure is that you occasionally receive preferential treatment and stuff that someone without this status would have to work a lot harder to obtain. It's common practice, but, for example, certain people are given things complimentary just because they are notable. And that's not totally unfair. I offered to buy a drink for James McNew of the band Yo La Tengo once simply because I loved Yo La Tengo. It's a gesture of appreciation.

But sometimes, it's a quid pro quo. As in, commerce plays a role. When a company sends a free pair of shoes to, let's say, Ryan Phillippe, that company hopes he will wear those shoes while being photographed having an affair on his wife and the shoe company will benefit from the ensuing scandal. Or maybe they just hope he'll be photographed wearing them to his gym—the gym he is probably having an affair at. Ryan Phillippe has had a lot of affairs, I think. Celebrity affairs sell so many shoes.

I have sometimes benefitted from being a small-time celebrity. I have been bought many drinks. I received a free bicycle seat from a bike shop in New York City. Also, once the attendant at the IKEA ferry in Manhattan let me cut the line. And, most notably, a hotel employee in Boston arranged, without my prompting, free porn for my room.

"Hey, Jon, I got you free porn!"

"Umm . . ."

"Yeah, it's just a switcher. All the porn movies on the hotel channel will play now . . . for free!"

"Oh, no, that's not necessary."

"Already done, man. Enjoy."

That's when you know you've made it. Free porn. Porn given to you just because someone likes your work. What a gesture of solidarity for someone in the arts community.

So, I watched. It would have been rude not to. Just as

a side note, the movie I watched that night starred a male actor with a particularly memorable penis, in that it bent upward. Later, I learned this may be a medical condition called Peyronie's disease. That's what free porn can teach you. Or any porn for that matter.

Anyway, he did have one (a bent penis), and no more than a week later, a happy coincidence occurred when I was at the baggage claim area of an LA airport. Just a short distance away stood the porn actor with the bent penis! As our eyes met, he knew I recognized him and looked away dismissively.

As I was staring, I quickly realized that male porn actors must hate their fans, because such a large percentage of their fans are sad, middle-aged men who watch porn all the time. It's not the best feeling to get thumbs-up from perverts all day. "Hey, love your bent penis!"

I wanted to tell him I was different, and about the free porn, and the unusual circumstance of my getting it—how I wasn't just another sad, lonely porn fanatic—but it was too late to try to explain. He and his bent penis got into a taxi and rode away into the hot LA night. Maybe I was reading it all wrong, and he recognized me and hated my work. It will be forever a mystery.

One of my good friends, David Cross, is a comedian who, over the years, has taken me to many baseball games. He is a big baseball fan and would often get complimentary tickets when the Red Sox (our team) played the Yankees. So, when the opportunity came for me to receive free tickets to Yankee Stadium, I was eager to return the favor.

Now, I had not ever received free tickets to a game before, so it was a momentous occasion. And here's how it went down. At the time, I was in a cartoon called *Home Movies* where I voiced a belligerent elementary school soccer coach named John McGuirk. Scott Van Pelt, an ESPN sports announcer, was a fan of the character, so he contacted me to do some comedy spots as Coach McGuirk to be played as interstitial segments on his new radio show for ESPN, which had just been acquired by ABC.

I recorded a rant about Tiger Woods seeming too clean and virtuous to be believed and that it was clear he was hiding some sort of dark sex-fueled secret life. This was around 2006. Scott Van Pelt wrote me after hearing it, saying ABC was uncomfortable with the content, because I mentioned Tiger Woods and sex too much. It was perfectly reasonable for ESPN to protect themselves from libel, but my fake coach character did technically break the Tiger Woods scandal story three years before it was revealed in the media. That's pretty good sports reporting from a cartoon character.

Anyway, my payment for the gig was tickets to a Red Sox game at Yankee Stadium, which Van Pelt said he could obtain with no problem, even though they couldn't use the material I gave them. He sent me the tickets, and I called David and boasted that I had gotten free Red Sox/Yankees tickets from ESPN. I added they must be some really good seats because on the tickets, it read something along the lines of "Special Seating."

We took the subway up to Yankee Stadium, and when we got in, I handed the tickets to the usher, who looked at them curiously. He stood there for a moment and then radioed someone. I was pretty confident at this point that my tickets were pretty impressive. I mean, the guy had to radio his boss. These were likely some VIP, press-credential seats. We would probably be hobnobbing with Giuliani and Bernie Kerick, eating free *plateau de fruits de mer.* I winked at David, believing I had set him up better than he had ever done for me.

Another usher came over and looked at the tickets, and the two, seemingly stumped, looked at each other. He radioed for a third usher to come over. Now, three people were looking at the tickets. Maybe we had field passes or were going to be brought to the locker room. Something big was brewing.

Finally, the third usher said, "Yeah, I know where these are, follow me." This was the old Yankee Stadium, so we were standing in the section behind home plate under the overhang (the original Yankee Stadium had a huge overhang which draped over the seating running from the second tier over about half the seating area directly behind home plate) and he walked us back up the stairs into the corridor where the food vendors were.

We walked for a minute or two until we reached an area in the hallway to the side, like an inset space set back from the main interior corridor in between two of the food vendors that had faded paint lines and about ten folding chairs in front of a cutout opening in the concrete wall. Through the cutout, the view was mainly the underside of the overhang, home plate, and the pitcher's mound.

I would classify it as an aggressively obstructed view of the playing field. I would also classify it as sitting in a hallway. I would definitely classify it as "Special Seating."

The usher said, "Here you are." David looked at me sideways. The folding chairs were in painted boxes reading one to ten and in front of us, within the walls of the actual stadium, through our cutout rectangular opening, was the handicapped seating area, to be fair. The seats were conveniently located for concessions, but it was almost impossible to see the field. It was like sitting in seats assigned for registered sex offenders. It felt as if we were on a practical-joke show. At least, that's what David assumed. A few feet behind us, people gathered in lines for food.

So now you understand the level of free gifts someone in my position receives. Free tickets to a hallway very near a baseball game. I sat in ignominy for the first few innings. I will say it was humbling, and a lesson learned that if you enter in a quid pro quo arrangement with Scott Van Pelt, don't settle on tickets.

After about three innings, two couples came in, dressed from head to toe in Yankees apparel—Yankees hats, Yankees shirts, even Yankees sweatpants. One of the women was even holding a Yankees flag.

As Red Sox fans, this was just adding insult to injury. Not only were we sitting behind a concrete wall, but now we'd been joined by really obnoxious Yankees fans. They were very loud and excited to be there. We struck up a conversation, and they kept reiterating what really big Yankees fans they were.

After a few minutes, we told them we were actually Red Sox fans. Then, one of the guys leaned over and said, "Wow, that's really good to hear. So are we. We drove from Vermont just to see the game and we've never been to Yankee Stadium before." We were very confused.

"Did you get these tickets from Scott Van Pelt?" I joked.

David asked them, "Why are you all dressed like that, then?"

The guy leaned in very conspiratorial, "We figured that as Red Sox fans, we would have to somehow find a way to blend in, so we went to the Yankees store and bought all this stuff to camouflage us."

"Wait, so you spent hundreds of dollars on Yankees gear because you thought you were going to get savaged by Yankees fans?"

"Yeah, like we said, we've never been to Yankee Stadium before. We heard it can get really bad for us. That's why we got the special seats. So we could be doubly protected."

This was some high level of conspiracy these Vermonters were pushing, a perfect companion piece to our seating woes. Of course the only other people in this area would be a group of people convinced they would be killed if they sat among regular folks in the stadium because they were rooting for the opposing team. Are baseball fans from Vermont really so cloistered from society that they believe Yankee Stadium was some sort of Thunderdome? Oh, Vermont.

After a few more innings, the Red Sox were way up, and my friend suggested we move into the stadium and sit in some open seats left by fans who left early. We said our goodbyes to the delusional folks from Vermont and watched the last two innings in pretty decent seats and left the stadium with the shared feeling that he and not I should provide any future tickets received for free.

Failed
Presidential Pets

Thomas Jefferson's Dog Buzzy

This briard, brought back from France, was, according to Jefferson, "one of the finest breeds" of farm dogs and was put to use as a sheepherder on Jefferson's farm. As a herder, Buzzy was responsible for wrangling the sheep, preventing them from straying outside the grazing area. Yet rumors of Buzzy having long-term sexual liaisons with one of the sheep were brought forward by some of the other sheepdogs. One dog claimed, "Buzzy would have relations with the sheep behind a tree while the other sheepdogs worked." Buzzy's litter did expose several puppies with extraordinarily fluffy fur, "not like a dog, but more like a sheep." Of course, there was a great deal of hemmings and hawings over Buzzy's indiscretion.

James Madison's Macaw

Madison, America's fourth president, was one of the founding fathers and architects of the Bill of Rights. But at the same time, Madison was a dedicated slave owner who kept hundreds of slaves at his Virginia plantation and proposed the three-fifths compromise, which counted slaves as three-fifths of a person for the purposes of apportioning representatives based on population. One anecdote from the Madison White House was that the parrot would be brought out to events on the shoulder of Madison's wife, Dolly, to proudly display the bird's ability to repeat phrases. But every time when asked, "Does Polly want a cracker?" The parrot would only reply with, "Yes, Polly wants a . . . ," unable to say *cracker*. This would cause much consternation for Madison and the guests, who all wanted the phrase to be repeated in full. After much debate and in some cases, heated arguments, a compromise was finally reached where they would stop asking Polly for the whole phrase and accepted her response as is. It became known as the three-fifths macawmpromise.

Andrew Jackson's Parrot, Poll

This parrot, an African gray, was brought to the White House as a gift for Jackson's wife and, unlike Madison's bird, had a real gift for mimicry. After Poll's introduction to the White House, many staff noticed that several of the indigenous birds on the grounds were being systematically exterminated. Bird after bird found dead, the bird bodies piling up, until there were no birds on White House grounds except for Poll. It was a mystery that confounded the president and the staff, until, one day, one of the White House groundskeepers claimed to have seen

Poll fly out of the executive residence window and bru-tally drive a family of finches off the property with a stick, then fly over and viciously beat a wren, then fly back through the window, maniacally laughing. Amos Ken-dall, the postmaster, overheard Jackson and Poll talking one day, as Poll ruthlessly made her infamous statement when describing her slaughter of a bevy of doves: "This is what it sounds like when doves die."

James Buchanan's Dog, Lara

This Newfoundland was a constant companion to Presi-dent Buchanan, as he was and remains to this day the only bachelor president in the White House. But Presi-dent Buchanan could be suffocating, and this had detri-mental effects on Lara's mood. On a two-week trip up north, Buchanan was readying for the trip back to Wash-ington and Lara apparently refused to board the train. Buchanan ordered her to heel, but she just sat on the tracks. Many of the people gathered around found it curi-ous, as did the president. It was inferred that this was a sign that Lara wanted to stay in Illinois without her owner, but Buchanan stated that dogs have "no rights which man was bound to respect."

Lara looked at him, like "I'm not moving, asshole."

Buchanan kneeled down and looked Lara straight in the eyes and said, "In my opinion, Lara, the legislation and histories of the times, and the language used in the Declaration of Independence, show that neither the class of species who had been imported . . . nor their descendants, were then acknowledged as a part of the people, nor intended to be included in the general words used in that memorable instrument . . . They had . . . been regarded as beings of an inferior order, and altogether unfit to associate with people, either in social or political relations; and so far inferior, that they had no rights which man was bound to respect; and that . . . might justly and lawfully be reduced to slavery for his benefit."

Lara stood her ground.

"Do you want a civil war?" Buchanan barked.

Lara, shaken by his tone, resigned and boarded the train. From that point forward, though, Lara knew a change needed to come.

Rutherford B. Hayes's Mastiff, Duke, and His Cat, Siam

In the beginnings of American industrialization, Hayes oversaw a great deal of infrastructure expansion during his tenure as president. His dog Duke was no stranger to that. Being a British mastiff, Duke was accustomed to a high standard. As Duke aged, he became larger and more phlegmatic, and was increasingly frustrated by the length of the walk from the solarium, where he used to lounge in the day, to the kitchen, where he was fed his ground lamb giblets. He loved his ground lamb giblets. In fact, he loved them so much, Duke added a meal between breakfast and lunch so as to eat more, but the added walk was affecting his mood. Along with John "Jack" Casement, chief engineer of the Union Pacific railroad, he designed tracks that would run from the solarium through the center hall, down the stairs next to the music room, through the basement hall to the kitchen. Once the plan was completed, Duke approached Siam, who had just arrived at the White House via Hong Kong.

"Despite your slight and slender constitution, you are to build me this railway track, so I am less taxed to receive my feedings," Duke told Siam.

Siam asked, "What's in it for me?"

Duke replied, "Nothing."

Siam reluctantly built the tracks, and the first trans–White House railway was completed.

Warren Harding's Dog, Laddie Boy

The Gilded Age is remembered by many as a time of extravagant wealth and a willful disregard of the underclass. Laddie Boy knew this dynamic all too well but was loyal to his master. He came from modest means but turned his back on this upon getting a taste of the sweet life. And that went for his sexual appetites as well. As he used to say, when asked about the poor of the country, "Mine is not to reason why, mine is just to 'eat that pie.'" Yes, Laddie Boy was quite the lothario, and his exploits were known throughout Washington. He took many lovers, as did Harding, and together, they were a rakish duo. Harding referred to Laddie Boy as his "wingdog" and together they were known to hold infamous sex orgies in what was called the "Dog House," which also happened to be the actual White House doghouse. Much effort was given to maintain the secrecy of these illicit affairs, which was why Harding and Laddie Boy insisted on all participants, dogs and women, to wear masks and enter with a password (Fido-lio). It has been estimated that Laddie Boy slept with more than twenty thousand dogs and some ten women in his lifetime.

Herbert Hoover's Dog, King Tut

Hoover was known as a fair-minded bureaucrat, but his administration was quickly saddled with the crippling economic devastation that was the Great Depression. Families were devastated, unemployment was at an all-time high, and people all over were desperate. Also, Prohibition ruled the land. Hoover called Prohibition "a noble experiment." But it caused a huge surge in organized crime, and not everyone believed in the experiment. King Tut was squarely in that camp. Much of the illegal activity during Prohibition involved bootlegging or rum-running, but King Tut got involved early in "pant-legging" or "leg-humping," which many dogs were recruited into at the time. Pant-legging was a diversionary tactic used by bootleggers. Dogs would be dispatched to hump the legs of the Bureau of Prohibition agents while the liquor deliveries were made. King Tut was the head of a particularly effective group of dogs known as the

Touchables, who were aggressive in their tactics and made it possible for the smuggling of millions of gallons of illegal liquor to speakeasies up and down the East Coast.

Harry Truman's Dog, Feller

Truman is attributed as saying, "If you want a friend in Washington, buy a dog." Well, he didn't, but one was sent to him as a gift: a cocker spaniel named Feller. But Truman was not a dog lover and never really wanted Feller around. There was much discussion of whether to get rid of Feller or keep him. Truman believed that getting rid of him would send a message that the acquisition of future dogs would be strongly discouraged. But some felt that it would be more humane to just keep him and deal with the repercussions. Truman felt getting rid of him, even though many would suffer, was a demonstrable show of force the likes of which no one had ever seen before. Instead of hearing from more dog lovers, Truman put Feller in a box labeled LITTLE DOG in the dead of night, flew him six hours away, and air-dropped him so that it would be too far for Feller to find his way back. Many felt that what Truman did was wrong, but no dogs ever returned to the Truman White House.

CHAPTER 18

Buying a Motorcycle (and How I Failed to Ride It)

I've had a long, failed history with transportation. My mother brags that I learned to walk very early, but on the whole, most of my other forays into different modes of transportation have been problematic. When I turned sixteen, my father bought me my first car. It was nice of him. It was a bumblebee-yellow MG Midget. I don't remember asking for it. Maybe it was one of those gifts that was really more for him than for me. Not that I didn't like it, but it was a bit much, in that cars are sometimes outward expressions of the personalities of the people who drive them. For example, if you drive a huge pickup truck with big-ass exhaust pipes jutting up from the cab and bumper stickers that read WHITE LIVES MATTER and JESUS HATES OBAMA, you just might be a redneck, or a really lazy liberal who bought a used pickup. You don't want to stand in opposition to the aura of your vehicle or contraindicate. It's too confusing.

Most people respect these norms and have a car that suits their personality. But many people overcompensate and overreach. Some people who lack self-confidence will buy big, fancy vehicles as a proxy for their lack of inner self-worth. Or big motorcycles, or big dogs, or big coats.

I've always wanted to make enough money to buy the world's biggest boat, just so I could name it—*Overboard*. But most overcompensations are small-scale efforts, like that time I wore a puka-shell necklace when I was fourteen for about a year and pretended that I was into surfing. But in the case of the MG, despite the fact that it was a tiny car, I could barely see over the wheel and it attracted a ton of attention, which was anathema to my personality. My inner car was more of a Plymouth Horizon, or, at best, a Honda Accord—one that doesn't attract gawkers.

Driving an MG compels the driver to conform to the notion that he or she is the kind of person who drives an MG. That kind of person is probably a college history professor or an ex–British MP, not a Jewish kid in high school. But like I said, sometimes you overreach or you're forced to.

About ten years ago, I bought an old dirt bike on eBay. It was one of those impulse buys. I thought a dirt bike would be a useful thing to have in New York City, because I often have to travel from the West Village to the

East Village to go to bars, and this would make the trip far more convenient and exponentially less safe.

I don't want to pass the buck, but Amy also had something to do with it. She obsessively bid on stuff on eBay— vintage clothing, area rugs, and, once, a pencil drawing by an eleven-year-old girl of Lance Bass lying in a field with a pony. (She won it for $12, and it's disturbing and beautiful.) So, in a way, she was my conduit to eBay.

I found an old Kawasaki that looked nice and won a bidding war that escalated the price to something like $900. When it comes to financial transactions, I have a hard time with confrontation, so if I walk into a store— let's say a furniture store—and I'm looking at a chair and a salesperson casually approaches, I immediately buy the chair, almost before they even speak. It's the "I'll take it" theory of economics. Or "laissez-faire carelessness." It's why I have close to 5,000 chairs. This goes for eBay, a terrible milieu for my condition, which involves almost unconscious clicking to bid more.

This problem with having no sense of financial limits has bled into my comedy life. Early in my career, I performed at this small venue on the Lower East Side in a show called *Eating It*. It was a showcase show, with a bunch of stand-ups performing short sets for $20. I was not exactly rich at the time. I mean, I could pay my rent, but $20 wasn't meaningless. I used to perform in a duo with a comedian named Mike Lee and our performing moniker was, cleverly, "Mike and Jon." But this partnership right away cut my $20 take by half. For one particular show, we decided that we would hire male escorts to perform live sex acts in our place. It was one of those ideas that I knew would make four to six people in the audience very happy and the rest very uncomfortable.

So the host would introduce Mike and Jon, and then, in lieu of us, two male erotic dancers in T-shirts, one reading "Mike" and the other reading "Jon," would go on stage and perform sex acts to music. Surprise! Arguably not comedy, but certainly not devoid of value, until you enter into, as it turns out, the very complicated world of gay escorts.

I started with a gay escort agency pulled off the back of the *Village Voice*. From there, I secured two men who were interested in the gig, for the fee of $300, plus an additional "manager" fee. So far, so good. I believed it was worth it, even for a show in the back room of a bar, for, at most, fifty unsuspecting people. I gave out the information, and Tony, the manager at the agency, told me they would contact me with the details once they secured the dancers.

After a few hours, I received a call from a guy named Frank. He said he was one of the dancers Tony called about the comedy-show gig. Frank asked me if I was interested in working independent of the agency because Tony takes a huge cut of the gig money. If agreed, he told me to call the agency and cancel the gig. I'm a democratic socialist, so I am always in favor of labor over usurious management practices. I told Frank that I was good with his plan.

A few hours passed, and then I got a call from a guy named Luan, who sounded Brazilian. He asked if I was the one who spoke to Frank after talking to Tony about booking two dancers. I was getting the sense that I was about to be enmeshed in a very complicated arrangement, admittedly one that I should have known might have happened when dealing with the world of low-end adult entertainment. Luan told me that he spoke to Tony about the gig, but he was curious why Frank called directly. He figured he should call Tony at the agency, because he was suspicious that Frank, who, according to Luan, was prone to erratic behavior, was trying to scam the agency. Classic good gay escort/bad gay escort. I told him I didn't want to get between them and would maybe try another agency.

Then Tony called. He had talked to Luan, and Luan tipped him off to Frank's chicanery. My main interest was to not talk to any more gay escorts or gay escort agents, and Tony was very mad at me. He told me that Frank couldn't work outside the agency, making it clear to me that Luan had flipped on Frank. Tony said he was trying to run a good, clean operation, and that Frank was compromising that by getting client info from the agency, then contacting the client directly and telling them to cancel with the agency. I explained that all I wanted was a couple guys to perform gay sex acts on stage for five minutes, and any way that could come to fruition, I was on board. Lots of serious shit going down at Gay Apple Escorts.

The night of the show, we were to meet Frank and Luan at a bar across from the venue to go over the plan for the show. Luan showed up, but Frank was late. Luan was tall, lean, and buttery-brown complexioned with straightened black hair, like second-album Prince. Frank was a wild card based on the phone calls, as you know, so we were worried that he wouldn't show, but he did. He was not what I expected: very plain-looking, almost suburban, like Joe Piscopo. As I started describing the bit, telling them they would both enter the stage after we were introduced and then they could just start playing out their gay sex act, Frank quickly spoke up.

"I'm not gay."

Silence.

"Umm . . . okay."

"Yeah, I'm not gay, so this is a problem."

"But I got you from a gay escort service?"

"Yeah."

"And I told you about the bit, so I assumed . . ."

"Well, yeah, but now that I'm here"—he pointed at Luan—"I'm not comfortable with this. I'll dance with him, but I'm not doing stuff with him."

I was a little stumped, and the show was in like ten minutes, and slightly panicked, because without the live gay sex part, it wasn't much of a bit. And it didn't seem like a sustainable plan to completely refuse the job you're hired to do, but how do I negotiate with him considering the nature of it? It was a real crocodile's dilemma, or, in this case, what is referred to now as the gay escort paradox.

How is a gay escort not gay if he is a gay escort? I asked Luan if he could call anybody he knew, and he scolded me. "I told you, you should have gone through the agency."

"Maybe for two hundred extra I would do it," Frank chimed in.

So Frank, who I had grown to trust over the course of these few days, finally showed his true colors. I knew it was too late to stop now.

"One hundred dollars," I countered.

"Deal."

The bit went off and was a real litmus test to the idea that people do not like to be surprised with live sex acts. Many people walked out, and as for Frank not being gay, it was never established, although him performing oral sex in front of fifty people certainly looked gay. Maybe I was being scammed all along. I did notice they glanced at each other during our pre-meeting in a way that made me think they knew each other before and had schemed the classic "I'm not gay" gay escort con. On the financial side, however, the bit ended up costing $500 and I made $10 back, so this speaks directly to my financial prowess. Always in the red.

So you can imagine the motorcycle purchase on eBay didn't go smoothly, either. After I won the bid, I read down the page for the details others might have noticed first: that the bike would have to be shipped to me, and that this would cost $400, because it was coming from Iowa. Iowa is in the Midwest and a great distance from New York.

I like to involve my sister, Jodi, in most of my "deals," so I decided to have it shipped to her house, outside of New Haven. A few weeks passed, and I arrived in Connecticut to welcome my dirt bike from Iowa. An eighteen-wheeler pulled into my sister's driveway. This was semi-exciting (pun). Then the driver got out and unloaded a pallet with not one but two dirt bikes. I tried to figure out how someone could accidentally send someone an extra motorcycle, but the driver of the truck didn't want to discuss it. Later, the owner would email to explain that he decided to throw in an extra, nonworking bike for parts to fix the working one. It was a fixer-upper's dream.

Unfortunately, I can't fix anything. Also, I know nothing about motorcycles. Also, neither bike worked.

With the reluctant help of my sister, I found a local handyman to see if he could get either of them running. He couldn't, but he said that for a small sum, he could truck one of the bikes to a New Haven dealership for repair. Now, two months after my eBay victory, I was in for an additional $400.

Then the dealership called. They had it working—another $150.

I went back to Connecticut to pick it up. I was excited. Soon, I would be on my iron stallion. As I paid, the repair guy informed me that I couldn't ride the bike because it was not "street ready." It needed signal lights, headlights, etc., which would cost in the range of $300 more to install.

I didn't want to spend any more money on it, so I called the handyman, and for some more money, he trucked the bike back to my sister's. I was now hovering around the $1,800 mark, and I had yet to ride my vintage eBay dirt bike.

Not long after, I went to my sister's for Passover. I decided I didn't care if the bike was street ready. It was a motorcycle. It was Passover. It was time to put the rubber to the road. I started it up and put it in gear and rode to the gas station to fill the tank. For all my money spent, here was the reward. That unparalleled feeling of man and machine, entwined in singular purpose. I gassed it up, got back in the saddle, and pulled out of the station, directly in front of a police car. I pretended not to see it, feigning confidence. But the cruiser abruptly made a U-turn and hit his lights. I rode, dejected, the one hundred yards or so to my sister's driveway. The cop wrote up the $200 ticket as my family and girlfriend all glared at me from the window.

That was the last time I rode my vintage dirt bike that I won on eBay and waited three months for. Total rubber-to-the-road time: forty-five seconds. The only positive thing to come of it was that I made the crime blotter in my sister's small-town paper for driving an unregistered motorcycle without a license, with an additional charge of riding without the proper signals. In a town like my sister's, that makes me infamous. I'm sure families are still gathered around their tables retelling the story about the mysterious stranger on the dirt bike. In the end, I guess I will think twice before bidding on eBay again, although I am interested in buying a submarine.

CHAPTER 19

Midnight Pajama Jam
(or How I Failed at Launching
a Kids' Show)

Not everything in my career has been successful. But sometimes failed endeavors hold the best memories. In comedy, as with everything, there is so much out there, unheeded, left aside, millions of moments just drawn and forgotten. Every piece of comedy, a stand-up set, a homemade sketch, a cartoon drawing, or a notebook of ideas—all that which lives on some abandoned corner of the internet or in some cardboard box, it will probably never be seen. It's what makes it special. It's a piece of personal history.

Back in the early 2000s, I was in a bit of a rut. I had just had a kid (the shit eater), and I was essentially out of work, except for a few acting roles here and there. At this point, with Amy's help, I came up with a concept for a TV show: a late-night talk show for kids called *Midnight Pajama Jam*. The goal would be to air the show around eight thirty or nine, around the time young kids go to bed, and make it like their version of *The Tonight Show*, except with absurdist guests.

An artist friend made two puppets, a purple octopus and an eagle, and I tapped comedian Jon Glaser to play the sidekicks—except instead of any puppeteering, he would just hold the two puppets up on his fingers and do the voices for both, unconcealed to the audience. The eagle, named Lumpy, had a gravelly tough voice and said "Raaaaaaaahr" a lot, and on the index finger of the other hand was the octopus named Scott Fellers, who had an effete accent, like Gore Vidal if he were an interior decorator.

The dynamic was that Lumpy and Scott Fellers disliked each other very much and would openly bicker all the time. As far as guests, we would come up with characters, a mix of random oddballs who would do traditional interview segments, but improvised based on an outline of some particular comedy conceit. It was a bit *Pee-wee's Playhouse*-ish, in that it completely ripped off *Pee-wee's Playhouse*.

We first set out to do a live test of the show in a small theater in Midtown in the afternoon to cater to an audience of mostly kids. We had a house band and three guests. One of the guests was a character called Pit Stain. He was a fictional "neighbor" who would drop by the show uninvited and tell mundane stories, with his hands always raised behind the back of his head, exposing the namesake pit stains. Next was a segment called "Vanity Plate," in which two guests who ostensibly had the same vanity plates on their respective cars come on. The plates read

HOT-STF; the man had it because he thought he was attractive, and the woman had it because she owned a bakery.

Everything in the show went fairly smooth until we presented a guest called Wyatt Trash, which was a bit where the actor Matt Walsh, dressed in overalls, sang a song with a Southern twang, with lyrics that went as follows . . .

> *I'm Wyatt Trash, I'll kick your ass*
> *I fucked your best friend's wife*
> *Eat a can of beans, drive to New Orleans,*
> *Now I'll try and suck my own dick.*

Then, he dove on the floor, and, awkwardly and with great effort, tried to contort his body to give himself oral sex. I don't know how we felt that this was okay, but it was, in retrospect, a glaring oversight, bordering on child abuse.

The upside was that most or all of the kids were too young to decipher what was happening and just laughed hard at a man writhing wildly on a floor without context. The problem was that the parents were not children and understood very clearly the context. So it was a bit of a moral conundrum. In hindsight, it was a show that adults and kids could enjoy together, as long as the kids didn't understand auto-fellatio.

As we developed the show, we phased out the kid angle and adapted it to be more strictly for adults but kept the puppets and the loose, wacky concept. This involved losing the full band and replacing it with my friend Gary behind a keyboard in a C-3PO mask, who'd mimic playing John Williams's theme from *Star Wars* as the CD was played over the sound system. We would still bring out fake guests with different comedy concepts and kept the improvisational nature of the show.

The odd thing about a failed venture is that, while you're working on it, you have no idea it's failing. I think we all thought at the time that we were on the cusp of something. At the onset, the show was exciting to do, despite audiences that topped off at about ten. When there are more people in the cast than in the audience, it makes for an odd dynamic.

We initially performed the show at midnight at the original UCB Theatre in New York City. The first show there had about eight people in the audience, and our guest musical act was the Trachtenburg Family Slideshow Players, who were a real family musical group (mother, father, and daughter) who wrote songs based on slides they found at estate sales, which they projected behind them when they sang. The daughter, who played drums, was around eight.

Gary, our C-3PO-masked bandleader, had taken acid that first night and got it in his head that the mother and the father were holding the daughter captive and making her play drums against her will, so during their performance, he tried to stop them by sticking his head through the curtain and trying to get the daughter's attention so he could free her from playing. Fortunately, he never ran

out and grabbed her. I guess even on acid, he was respectful of boundaries.

When we started to do the show weekly, we performed it
at the UCB Theatre in Chelsea, right around the time it
moved there from its original location. That theater had
about one hundred seats and had taken over the space from
a small repertory theater. The most interesting shows were
the ones where the audience (for our show) was split between
a smattering of friends and then a few older couples who
thought they'd be seeing a show staged by the previous repertory theater and never checked that the theater had
changed to an improv comedy venue. I'm not certain which
I enjoyed more: the disdain from children's parents or the
disdain from confused old folks wondering why they were
seeing Wyatt Trash and not *Hedda Gabler*. Although there
were parallel Freudian themes.

As we kept doing the show, our audience didn't exactly
swell. It more just smoldered. Typically, with this kind of
project, you see some returns for your efforts, as word of
mouth would start to spread and audiences would start
growing in size. And I'm not saying there wasn't incre-
mental progress, but on the whole, most shows were not
well attended. But this wasn't exactly unfamiliar territory.

Once, when I was in a sketch troupe in Boston called
Cross Comedy, we came to New York City to do a run at a
small theater in a Midtown black box theater, and the first
show's audience consisted solely of my aunt. Literally, only
my very Jewish aunt Marion, sitting at a front-row table basically touching the stage. The rest of the room was empty.

We noticed this only moments before the show because we were all in the green room, and then one of the members of the group went to check out the crowd and returned to say, "You all will want to see this." When we discovered the empty theater but for the older woman in the front, and I recognized that older woman as my aunt Marion, I begged them to consider canceling, but we were rehearsing for an industry show (to present to television executives) so the rest of the group insisted on doing it.

The comedian Dave Attell was the warm-up act, and he had to go out and do ten minutes of stand-up exclusively for my aunt, who, by the time we started our show, was eating a Reuben sandwich with a glass of red wine at her table.

After the show, she said stolidly, in her very Jewish voice, "I liked the comedian." So not only did we just perform only for my aunt, but she ended up not even liking it. So yes: I'd had some experience with dismally attended shows.

Sometimes, in comedy or any other endeavor self-promoted and self-sustained, just sticking around is half the battle. So many unbelievably funny people dropped out of doing comedy, simply because it's a zero-sum game at a certain point. I just happened to be lazy enough to not get out of it. Basically, I hung around long enough.

But *Midnight Pajama Jam* was wearing out its welcome, so Jon Glaser and I did the natural thing and decided to gather enough money to make a DVD despite strong public disinterest. It was like the *Producers* scheme except everybody, including us, would lose money. I got donations from friends and family, and we staged a show taped at a small theater called the Marquis in downtown NYC.

The show went well. We had Matt Walsh back as Wyatt Trash. The comedy duo Slovin and Allen came on portraying two fundamentalist pastors who travel the country warning kids of the evils of pornography from the back of a van. Also, Eugene Mirman came on dressed in period costume as a "gayhunter," in the spirit of Van Helsing, but instead of vampires, he hunted gay people. Also, comedian Sam Seder, who happened to have really huge and muscular calves in real life, held up a curtain, with his back to the audience, and set a spotlight toward the bottom of it and, as music came on, raised the curtain to reveal his oiled-down calves, like some fetish striptease. If nothing else, we finally captured the essence of a show that we had worked on for the better part of three years.

It was a bit of a mess, but it was a creative, ambitious mess. And the taping gave us hope that we could sell the show to television so we could get a bigger audience on board. That would pay back our small investors (my sister, Jodi) and put us in a position to achieve bigger goals. We couldn't wait to get to editing the footage we had.

In fact, our editor Bill Buckendorf called the next day and told me to come over to his apartment as soon as I could. Apparently, he was as excited as I was to get this show together. Bill did all the videos for *Midnight Pajama Jam*. He lived in the East Village on St. Mark's in a six-story walk-up, so I was never excited to go over there to edit, but knowing we had done a good show overshadowed my hatred of climbing six flights of stairs.

I got there and sat down at his desk in his small bedroom, where he edited. He looked a bit sheepish, as if something was wrong. I asked if he was all right. He gestured to the monitor and said that I "should see for myself." He played down the raw footage of the show's opening and there was no sound, so I told him to turn it up.

He said, "It is up. There's no sound."

"On the whole thing?"

"No, not the whole thing."

"Oh, thank God."

"The sound kicks in at the very end."

"At the very end of all the footage?!"

"Yeah."

"FUCK!"

"I think the sound guy forgot to press record until the very end of the show."

After all this, our record of the *Midnight Pajama Jam* show is basically a silent movie until I come out to say good night to the audience. I suppose it was a poetic climax to a show that maybe was never meant to be, and a testament to the idea that some of the best memories are the times leading up to the grandest failures. I'm sure that's how the guys at Enron felt, but, in our case, all we did along the way was lose money. We were poor but happy. Well, not exactly happy.

Failed Business Ideas

Jon Benjamin's 911

Instead of calling 911 directly, call me first and let me be the first voice you hear in an emergency situation. I will assess, take notes and listen to every detail, and then immediately pass on your info to the real 911. Despite it taking a little extra time in a potentially time-sensitive crisis, it will be worth your while to be comforted by the molasses-y smooth tones of my rich and soothingly soulful voice.

White Coffee

The most expensive coffee in the world is called Kopi Luwak. It is coffee that has been collected after being eaten and digested, then expelled (as in shit out) by the civet, a wild cat indigenous to Indonesia. It sounds disgusting, but supposedly it adds to the richness and complexity of the taste. It costs around $50 a cup. My concept is based on the Indonesian model, but *Americanize* it. Take standard beans, have American-born white children eat them, digest them, and shit them out, then process them to make White Coffee. The difference in taste and pride and the even more unusual production process really puts this cup above all the others. Based on the small batch of white children used to make White Coffee, the cost of a cup would be around $250.

Slide-oos

Shoes that slide. Slide-oos are shoes with specifically designed carbon fiber sheets attached under them to make walking less leg intensive. Most of walking involves lifting the legs, but Slide-oos change all that by just adjusting the design. With Slide-oos, you shuffle and slide more and walk less, expending less energy and creating more fun. Sliding is more fun than walking. It's always been. And Slide-oos are built to slide. How many people out there would rather slide to work every day than walk? I bet a lot. Think back to when you were a kid. One of the best things to do after a big snowstorm was get up early, go out, and slide on the ice. Slide-oos let you do this anytime, anywhere, and in any weather.

The Big Chair

Do you remember the feeling you had when you were a child? When everything seemed wondrous and new? When you were carefree and filled with endless optimism? When you sat in a chair and let your feet dangle above the ground? Well, you can experience all those feelings again with the Big Chair. The Big Chair is a regular chair designed 30 percent bigger to scale than a standard-size chair, so your feet can dangle, giving you the sensation of being young again. The Big Chair is an immediate mood elevator and natural relaxant. After a hard day at work or a hard day at home with the kids, sitting in a chair that's a little too big for you will make all the difference. Sometimes you just need to feel smaller to feel better.

Leftovers: the Restaurant

Food waste has always been a major issue at restaurants, and sometimes people eat less than half the food brought to them. Leftovers is a great place to eat and a great place to eat cheaply. Here's how it works. All Leftovers meals can be ordered at full price, but for people not queasy about sharing strangers' food, Leftovers provides the ability to order the remainders of other people's meals. Let's take, for example, our chicken parmigiana dinner with ziti and marinara on the side, priced at $16.95. That's a big plate of parm. At Left overs, depending on how much of it you have eaten, you may bid out your uneaten portion to another guest, who can buy it at a reduced price based on the amount of food left over. It's sharing at a reasonable cost. And Leftovers essentially pays you back for not eating as long as you can find another hungry customer who's not squeamish about hygiene. So, your $16.95 chicken parm just got down to $8 after you sell your leftovers, and so on.

With that, based on what you can bid out to others, your meal's cost goes down commensurate to what you've paid forward. It's a way to eat what you want and not feel bad about leaving what you don't.

Cool Shades

Sunglasses have always been at the forefront of "cool." Cool Shades are sunglasses you can put on anything to make it cooler, not just on your face. Cool Shades are custom-size according to your specific needs depending on exactly what you want to make look cooler. Put them on your dog, and you've got a "cool dog." Put them on your lamp, and you've got a "cool lamp." Put them on the tank of your toilet, and you've got a "cool toilet." Put them on the front of your car, and you've got a "cool car." Even put them on the casket at your grandpa's funeral, and you've got a "cool funeral"! On anything, anywhere, Cool Shades make it cool.

Laius Grove—a Unique Resort Adventure—"Luxury with a Twist"

Vacations are becoming more and more specific. These days, you can plan a trip around very particular interests, like yoga, vegan cooking, glamorous camping, water sports, even as micro-focused as martini resorts that cater to those who want a completely immersive experience in learning about and drinking martinis. I have come up with a resort experience that has appeal for those travelers whose spirit of adventure draws them in a different, more unique direction. Here is the brochure.

Elegant Accommodations

Retreat to your finely appointed room or suite with a tropics, garden, pool, ocean, or ocean-front view. Each features a spacious living area, a full bathroom with Jacuzzi, your own furnished terrace or balcony, a complimentary minibar, and more.

World-Class Spa

Treat yourself to dozens of pampering choices in the Laius Spa. Experience pure indulgence through a combination of the latest hydrotherapy and indigenous treatments. Then grab a workout in our state-of-the-art fitness center.

Gourmet Dining

Indulge in an expansive array of international cuisines. Dine out at one of our à la carte gourmet restaurants, where reservations are never required. Enjoy fine wines, beers, and other top-shelf spirits in any of our bars, lounges, and restaurants. You can even order your favorite cocktail poolside or on the beach.

Weddings

Make your fairy-tale wedding come true at Laius. Choose from three romantic wedding packages, each featuring free anniversary nights. Our professional wedding coordinator can handle every detail, so you can focus on each other.

Kill Your Father

Laius Grove will customize a hunt to create a memorable experience for you and your family. Our professional staff will help coordinate, plan, and oversee the entire process, so you can enjoy the singular rewards of this most special of occasions. As we say, we do the work, you just kill your father.

CHAPTER 20

How I Failed to Have a Chinese Dinner While Visiting My Parents in Arizona

My parents, after their retirement, moved to Arizona for the winters. Traditionally, Jewish retirees ("snowbirds") would get a place in Florida, but my parents went against the grain. They decided on Tucson. It is a nice city. Temperate in the winter and surrounded by mountains, with an extensive network of desert walking trails in the foothills. My father and mother like to hike, so for them, this was the perfect spot. I did not inherit their love of walking. I abhor a walk. Well, I wouldn't totally say that, but I definitely resent a walk. I am conflicted. I'm sure I inherited the will to walk from them, but I am fighting that will at every turn. And I hate turning. In fact, the rejection of my parents' traits has been a prominent part of my identity.

My father is an active guy. Even when I was a kid, he was always doing something, whether it be home improvement work, some outside project, exercise, etc. As I remember him then, he was never at rest, constantly in motion. And my mother was a professional dancer, so the always-in-motion attribute similarly applied.

As my parents aged, this perpetual movement didn't end. Even when they bought a winter condo in New Hampshire for respite, there was never a sense of stillness. My father even started to build a stone wall running from the condo, down a forested hill. Stone by stone, he stacked a three-foot wall. Not for any purpose, like keeping out interlopers or marking a property line, just a random wall in the woods whose end was indeterminate. An eternal wall. It was like a Greek myth.

> **Boy:** What are you doing, Father?
> **Father:** Building a wall.
> **Boy:** Why?
> **Father:** To build a wall.

Me, I like a good, long sit. I think I developed that while watching them. I could watch someone work all day. I have an unquenchable thirst for apathy. That creates some tension between me and my parents, who may prefer their son work hard, in their image. But I do enjoy my trips to Tucson. It's a time to sit back, tense up, and be with family.

In 2006, the third year I was to visit them there, I received a phone call from my mother. She was excited for my trip, and knowing I had become something of a food lover during my time living in New York City, she told me they were excited to take me to a new restaurant they had discovered.

Now, before I get into this any further, I should explain that these trips to Arizona almost exclusively revolved around food. Yes, there was the hiking and the walking, but mainly the day began and progressed with planning and coordination and the discussion of dinner. Where? When? For restaurants that they had been to, a detailed accounting of prior meals there. How they've changed, or how the quality fluctuates.

And scheduling. The careful and critical precision that goes into deciding when to leave in order to make the reservation on time or slightly before, depending on whether there would be a drink at the bar. Nothing is left to chance. Discussion of lunch plans runs concurrent with the daylong, extended conversation about the upcoming dinner plans. So, as you can imagine, there were one to two balls in the air at all times.

There is a small, elite collection of choices of places to eat, all curated over time by my parents. There are maybe five to seven restaurants that they go to, and while the rotation may change, on every visit, like clockwork, we would hit each spot. On occasion, there would be talk about switching it up, but on the whole, my parents are creatures of habit. Oh, and also, they like dining out but are a little less particular about the quality of the food than your average refined diner. They are more into ambiance. And really overcooked chicken. I know it's a trope, but, if memory serves, there hasn't been an order of chicken that isn't sent back to be cooked "a little more, please." Cooked (a Little More, Please) should be the name of a restaurant for old people.

But when my mother called, she was quick to highlight that the place she and my father had discovered was a Chinese restaurant. She knows I like Chinese food, and during my time in New York City I had spent a great deal of time discovering the best under-the-radar places in Manhattan, Brooklyn, and Queens. My interest was immediately piqued, because I hadn't thought of Tucson as having a large Asian community, let alone a real Chinese food scene. Still, she reassured me that this place was remarkable, a "real gem in the rough." With that, I was on board. Any city in any locale can sprout a real "gem in the rough" type place, so I was into it.

A few days later, I received another call from her, and again, she mentioned the "gem in the rough," as they had eaten there the night before and she repeated how amped up they were about introducing me to this place . . . so authentic. So now, for accounting purposes, two mentions of the phrase "gem in the rough," which hadn't bothered me prior to the first phone call, but after the second, was now my least favorite phrase.

Before my flight, there was a third call, with a last-minute mention that we would eat at the "gem in the rough" the first night I arrived. So, to summarize, my parents were off-the-charts excited to impress me with this new hidden treasure, with some of the best, most authentic Chinese food in the Southwest.

I arrived in Tucson, took the obligatory hike, and promptly at six o'clock, we piled into the car to finally see what all the fuss was about. We drove for a while through a pretty remote part of north Tucson, until finally we turned a corner, where from the back seat I had a clear view of a long street and up ahead in the distance, a massive thirty-foot cheesy pagoda gate with horses, and on top a sign, lit up: P.F. CHANG'S. To its right, a massive parking lot with the warehouse-size restaurant, and next to that a Lowe's or some big-box store.

I almost swallowed my tongue. I think I even uttered a barely audible squeal. But at this point, I'm not sure whether this was the place they'd been touting or if there's still a shot we drive by it and continue on to "the gem in the rough."

"There it is," my mom said. Pregnant pause.

"P.F. Chang's?"

"Yup."

"Oh."

"It's delicious."

"But it's P.F. Chang's."

"Yeah."

"I mean, I know it, I just figured you guys were saying it was some little secret spot."

Then, my dad. "What do you mean you know it? It's a local Tucson place."

Dark clouds were gathering.

"I mean . . . no . . . P.F. Chang's is a big chain."

Then my dad slowed the car down and craned around. "No, it is not." This was declarative, not interrogative.

"Dad, there's a thirty-foot sign and the restaurant is the size of an airplane hangar. This is not a 'gem in the rough.' There's hundreds of P.F. Chang's. There's a few right outside New York City."

Then, my dad again, slowly: "You are mistaken."

"I'm not, trust me."

Then, him, gravely: "This is the only P.F. Chang's."

Now, at this point, it probably would have paid to be diplomatic, or at least employ some level of restraint. I knew he wanted to believe that P.F. Chang's was some personal discovery, but . . .

"Dad, you're very *wrong*. P.F. Chang's is basically a fast-food Chinese chain with probably thousands of locations all over the place. When we go in, I'll ask the non-Chinese hostess for the map of all the locations."

He went ashen. Fury. Silent fury filled the car. He jammed into a parking space and got out, with a look like if he could, he would wrap his hands around my neck and squeeze till I told him with a crushed larynx that there was only one P.F. Chang's and that he and my mother found it and—pointing at the restaurant—that was it. We took the short "dead man walking" walk into the restaurant in deafening silence. When we entered, it was your typical monster-size P.F. Chang's with not a single Asian employee, right down to the teenage white hostess I had predicted.

"Excuse me, do you have a map of your locations nationwide?"

I couldn't resist.

"We do."

She reached under her hostess station and pulled one out. It was a map with like five hundred red dots all over the country. My dad was seething.

"Table for three, please."

We ate our meal without much talking. I had the lo mein. It was decent. My dad had the humble kung pao.

For the remainder of the trip, my dad was embittered by what is now referred to as "Chang-gate," not to be confused with the actual Chang gate in front of most P.F. Chang's: that huge entrance gate that people pass through on their way to a really large Chinese chain restaurant with hundreds of locations all across the country.

To this day, we can't eat at P.F. Chang's without the sting of that moment rearing up—that moment when a father and son faced off in an epic struggle over truth, pride, and a side of oversteamed rice. If you ever happen to be in the Tucson area or the Birmingham area or the Huntsville area or the West Des Moines area or the Little Rock area or the Burbank area or the El Segundo area or the Atlanta airport area, or any number of other areas, you may want to check out this little "gem in the rough" called P.F. Chang's. Take your parents, even though they may see you as a curse on their very existence.

CHAPTER 21

The Flood: a Waste of Waters Ruthlessly (or How I Failed My Rental Car)

I f you don't know who I am by now, my main claim to fame is voicing the character Bob on the animated show *Bob's Burgers* and voicing Archer on the show *Archer*. These are two very popular animated shows on television, and being a cast member on them has been a big part of my life for the last ten years. At this point, my animated children are essentially the same age as my real-life one.

The shows have been part of my life and hugely beneficial. First, because, being an actor, at least prior to these jobs, was very up and down workwise, and since these shows have been on air for a long time, I have some job security; and second, because voiceover work makes for a very easy schedule. Unlike regular television acting, voice work is time-efficient for the actors. There is no "hurry up and wait." An episode of an animated show takes the actors only a few hours to record, as opposed to a live-action show, where one episode can take at least a week. I record both shows a few miles from my apartment and occasionally receive free tea from the café across from the studio just because my nasally voice is regularly on TV. Normal voices have to pay for tea.

Voice work was never a goal of mine when I was a young comedian. As a matter of fact, I never even really knew about how or why people did it when I auditioned for my first animated show in a pantry of a guy's kitchen in Cambridge, Massachusetts, where he had hung a microphone in front of shelves of canned goods. This wasn't some Disney soundstage. It was more like voice-over porn. I remember feeling dirty afterward. But that was more a product of having to perform oral sex on him for the job. That's how it works in the voice game.

The first show I worked on, *Dr. Katz, Professional Therapist*—the one I auditioned for in a closet—was a collaboration between the comedian Jonathan Katz and a science teacher turned software developer named Tom Snyder, who created an innovative way to make a comedy show, involving very cheaply produced animation and comedians recording their acts, with Katz portraying a therapist and chiming in. It was essentially comedians using their routines as a fake therapy session. I played the cartoon therapist's lazy son.

From this part, I started a career in voice work and

quickly learned I was singularly unsuited for the basic parameters of the job, which mainly consist of the ability to perform multiple voices. I can perform about two. Unless I'm forced, in which case I can do an old-Jewish-man voice and an old-man-from-Maine voice. But my career was reared in a world where it was more important to not pay extra talent, so I flourished.

Tom's company used a lot of "nontalent" to do voices, because it was more convenient than casting. So some voices in shows like *Home Movies* were people who worked in the company (the guy in shipping, for example) as opposed to actors. There were definitely a few times where I was asked to play a character that would have been dramatically better if a real voice actor was called in, but I was there. I often get asked how to get into voice work, and I usually say the best way forward is just get another job and hopefully someone will be producing an animated show nearby and they'll ask you to do a voice.

When I was cast to do the voice of Archer, I worked a whole season of the show without meeting a fellow cast member or the creators who cast me. This is not uncommon in voice work, wherein you record from anywhere, with the directors on the phone filling in for the other actors. So it's basically a puzzle piece in the process. This is, conversely, not how it works on *Bob's Burgers*, because the actors perform together more like live-action, all in the same recording booth, or via headphones if the other actor is in another city. But for *Archer*, there was a world where I would never meet any other people connected to the show, if not for publicity events.

Now, let me point out that publicity is my least favorite part of being on a television show, but it's also an integral part of the work. I guess all the shows I worked on that preceded *Archer* and *Bob's Burgers*, like *Lucy: The Daughter of the Devil* and *The Dick & Paula Celebrity Special*, were so under the radar that normal avenues of publicity were never taken, so I was not exactly prepared for talking about the shows I was in.

After season one of *Archer*, I was invited to participate in an annual publicity event put on by the Television Critics Association, the TCA Awards. It takes place over a two-week period in a resort in Pasadena, California, and all the new shows and existing shows are presented for the television critics via Q and A's with the shows' stars and creators. Each network gets a day to feature their shows, while the entertainment reporters sit in sequestration for two weeks, eating catered food and rolling in and out of consciousness while sitting from panel to panel.

I actually had done this one time before, for *Home Movies*, and as I remember, the reporters used our panel as a pee break—as in, when we took the stage, they left en masse, so we presented to a nearly empty room. When I received a call to attend the event in support of *Archer*, I declined. A few minutes later I got a call reminding me that I was the voice of Archer, so I needed to be there.

I was actually on vacation in Gloucester, Massachusetts, at the time, so this was already an imposition, but I
reluctantly agreed. They do fly cast members first-class,
and, to be honest, I had not traveled first-class that much,
so it was something of an incentive. I think that was one of
the selling points for going: "They'll fly you first-class."
First-class is very enticing. Imagine if the army flew everyone first-class; so many more people would enlist. The mil-
itary should at least offer an upgrade to people who'd pay.

I went to Logan airport in Boston and boarded my
flight, settling into my first-class seat, with an occasional
guilty glance back through the veiled curtain to the hard-
scrabble confines of coach. "I'll have the filet mignon," I
told the flight attendant. After my meal, I enjoyed copious
amounts of cabernet sauvignon and polished off an ice
cream sundae. I disembarked with a first-class smile and
nod to the flight attendant, while chewing on my complimentary mint, looking forward to a bright and prosper-
ous future ahead.

Now, for the failure portion of the story. I had taken
the last flight out to maximize my vacation time, so I got
in very late to LAX, and when I went to collect my rental
car, I had forgotten that it was a pretty long drive to Pasadena. I upgraded to a midsize and hit the road. It was
around midnight.

Now, for context, I declined the GPS, so I was basically winging it (Pasadena is about an hour-long drive
from the LA airport). As I was on the main highway

north, the exit I was to take was unexpectedly closed for repairs, so I was stuck on the highway with no idea how to get to Pasadena. I decided to take surface roads to figure it out.

About five minutes off the highway, it hit me. A deep-set bubbling gurgle from the upper stomach moved like a rotating fist into my lower bowels. A gusher. I clenched up knowing what was forthcoming. Fucking filet mignon in first class. The situation was progressing quickly, so I drove feverishly to the nearest gas station, slid out of my car as stiff as a paddleboard, and did an ass-clenched hop to the pay window.

"Bathroom?"

"No bathroom."

"Please, I'm sick . . ."

"No bathroom."

Fuck. More hopping back to my car. I slid back in and drove with my ass off the seat till I found another gas station nearby. Sweaty and white as a ghost, I did the clenched hop to another gas station attendant and got the same result. So, now with greater urgency, I shuffled back to the car for some much-needed strategizing. My walk was more of a sway, like a waltz performed by a marionette. Every ounce of energy was being put toward holding in the fetid contents of my first-class meal inside my anus.

So this was the moment of truth. The moment when I had to decide whether to go to the bathroom in a garbage can or on somebody's lawn. I drove slowly, scoping out lawns that had enough cover to sit and have diarrhea on for an indeterminate length of time. I was also in some serious distress, but not enough to consider the important issues: What happens after? What happens after I have diarrhea on a lawn for twenty minutes? What is the process by which I clean up? I would have to use my clothes.

Now, the decision in my very confused physiological state was between knocking on someone's door or giving all my effort to hold the diarrhea at bay till Pasadena and driving as fast as I could. I was now around Fairfax and Melrose, around forty minutes till Pasadena.

I went with the latter option, holding it, and I will explain for you why. It was akin to the scene in the M. Night Shyamalan movie *Signs*, where the wife was pinned by a car against a tree, but she was alive and lucid. This is called crush syndrome, whereby the object that has crushed the victim is actually keeping them alive, and when and if extricated, what is called "the smiling death" occurs, in which the rapid blood loss causes immediate death. I guess the smiling part is based on the idea that the person crushed is in a really good mood before the moving of the thing crushing them. My car seat was, in this analogy, that object. The pressure I was putting on my ass, by pressing it into the car seat, was holding in the inevitable shit storm. So my theory was that I needed the car to not go. I was one with the car now.

I just needed to get to Highway 101 and get to the hotel and then rush to the lobby bathroom. It was at least 1:30 a.m., so there were no cars on the road and I was confident now that I had a plan. The next fifteen to twenty minutes were critical. I had to dig deep to work some "mind over matter" techniques. The urge to release was excruciating, but I kept pressing. My left leg pushed as hard as it could against the seat floor of the rental car, putting me into a heavy lean to the right, whereby my left ass cheek was pressing my right with generous force, leaving just enough flexibility to control the gas pedal with my right foot. I was basically semi-slumped but still driving. I would have steered with my chin if necessary. Anything to not go.

Next, I started chanting. Specifically, chanting the word *fuck* over and over in different ways, as in sometimes sustained and baritone and sometimes high-pitched and squealed. It was like an impromptu fuck opera. This got me to the 101, which would take me to the 134 to Pasadena. Chanting full-voiced now in essentially a fugue state and also exhausted by the perpetual flexing of all the seven hundred or so muscles in my body, I hit the 134, and that was a huge benchmark. I saw the sign for Pasadena and it was like a puddle of water to a man dying of thirst.

Then, it happened. One cannot say who was to blame. I could blame the state of California or I could blame God, but I hit a huge bump, which set a rapid succession of events in motion. First, it caused me to swerve slightly, which forced me to release my positioning and my clench for just enough time for diarrhea to spew. It was simultaneously horrifying and immensely pleasurable. I knew at once that this was the end of one problem and the beginning of many more.

The immediate relief was quickly replaced with two concurrent issues: first, diarrhea in my shorts; and second, the need to have more diarrhea. So, at seventy-five miles per hour, I had to return to the crush syndrome position, but now in a puddle of poo. And, there's another thing about diarrhea in a very small, enclosed space: the wrenchingly awful odor. I opened the windows and returned to the *fuck* chanting, while in full clench at about eleven miles out from my exit.

I remember looking down and laughing maniacally at my choice of wearing shorts, because at least pants would have contained the mess. Also, with seepage, the car seat was getting the runoff. Fucking first class. A flash of my winking and doing a finger gun to the flight attendant ran through my mind. Things were so good back then, some two and a half hours before. Now, I was in a kiddie pool of shit. And the thing about it was, I was so close—I had come so far, just to be derailed by a bump. I finally made it to the exit and had to move into stage two of a strategy session with myself. My situation was very delicate.

I drove toward the hotel and pulled over in the secluded, upscale neighborhood where the resort was. I was about two minutes away from it, but I knew I had to do some cleanup before driving in. My plan: use my T-shirt to wipe up and put on clean clothes, at least getting semi-presentable (besides the stench) as I drive up.

But herein lay the rub. Getting up again. The move to the trunk would inevitably cause more problems than it would solve. But I had to change shorts, right? I mean, they were soused. I tried a slow rotation toward the door and knew better. I had to just accept the fact that I had to do this as is. I put the car back in drive and drove the remaining half mile to the hotel.

As I approached the gates, I shut off the headlights, like it was a heist. As bad as this was, I still had my dignity and wanted the best possible chance of doing this without drawing extra attention. My goal: to spy if the valet was there so I could pull up without being spotted. Then, I would get as close to the entrance as possible, jump out, grab my bag in the trunk and hightail to the bathroom inside, hoping to skirt anybody there.

It was around 2:00 a.m., so the hotel, from my vantage point, looked clear of any hotel staff. I went through the mental checklist again just to be certain—backpack then trunk then bathroom—then gunned the gas and made my move, causing a slight sloshing effect below in the seat.

Oh, and by the way, the poor seat. My rental car seat was really in dire shape, being all diarrhea-ed on and such. I jerked it into park and was reaching for my backpack in the passenger seat when I was startled by the sound of an opening door.

The valet. Right there, as if he had just materialized. Leaning over, full of shit, with my head craned around meeting eyes with him, I must have looked like a cornered, dying animal. His face showed all. A strange combination of earnest intention, shame, guilt, and hope, along with the strained smile of someone covering up the stark reality that something smells and looks incredibly rotten. Knowing I had no time to waste, I darted past him with my backpack, leaving the door open, and rushed into the hotel lobby.

The lobby was grand in scale and decor, and the registration desk was a good distance to my left. A man emerged behind the desk as I hobbled in at a swift pace and I just yelled out, "Bathroom?" Barely acknowledging where he pointed, I continued my harried move to salvation: a toilet, toilet paper, and running water. After some aimless rambling, I finally saw the dark wooden door. The finish line. The end of this Old Testament–style, punishing journey. Stripped naked in a stall, I spent the next five minutes finishing what I had started.

And then a sudden realization hit: I had left my bag in the trunk with all my clothes.

I spent a long sad moment staring at the pile of soiled shorts, boxer shorts, and T-shirt on the bathroom floor, knowing I had no options left. I just wanted to die now. Quietly exhale and die on the bathroom floor of the Langham resort in Pasadena, California. And let the crime scene cleaners come in and do what they do.

After several dozen heavy sighs, I sucked it up and began the grunt work of wiping down the shorts with toilet paper. I put them back on, figuring I would have to get back to my car, grab my keys and get my stuff, run back to the bathroom and change, and then, finally, check in to my room, where I could take a shower.

With great discomfort, I redressed in my diarrhea outfit

and began frantically cleaning up the scene as best I could, culminating in picking up the boxer shorts to throw out. When I left the stall, I saw there was no receptacle for garbage but instead one of those baskets because in place of paper towels, there was only cloth.

After all this, luxury (just like the first-class airline food) once again punched me in the gut with irony, and I was faced with the moral quandary of dumping a shit-soaked pair of boxers in a pile of towels for the cleaning person. Motherfucker, this wouldn't end. Having gone through the entire toilet paper supply, I decided to wrap the boxers in paper toilet seat covers to at least make an effort at mitigating the problem. I ran back and wrapped the boxer shorts like I was swaddling a baby.

While doing this, the door to the bathroom opened, and I jerked up to see a large security guard with his hand on a baton. I froze. And then it all became clear. I saw what he was seeing. Not long before, a heavy-set, balding middle-aged man had driven at a high rate of speed into the hotel entrance, bounded out of his car covered in diarrhea, and run into the hotel. And now, he found that person, standing in the bathroom holding a wad of toilet seat covers in his hands.

"I'm a guest at the hotel."

"Sure you are."

"Let me explain," I said.

He moved slowly toward me, because what else would anyone do?

"You need to come with me," he said.

What followed was a long, sad walk toward the lobby, the guard keeping me at a healthy distance with his baton, while I tried desperately to explain to him that I was sick and not insane. I even offered up my now shit-soaked license to prove I was a hotel guest. In the end, I was able to convince him of my story and I was checked into the hotel by some very kind and smell-tolerant clerks.

In the morning, as in about four hours later, I met the cast and creators of *Archer* for the first time and yawned my way through the event. After the panel, I called for my car, realizing I never even bothered to check it.

As I waited in the porte cochere (pretentiousness, remember?) for the valet to bring it around, I was mortified at the thought that some poor attendant had to drive it even the one hundred yards to the lot, given its condition. I mean, I had used my front seat as a diaper. Then the car pulled up and an attendant got out smiling.

"Mr. Benjamin." He gestured me in as he hopped out. I slowly poked my head in and took a whiff. Curiously, it smelled fresh and clean. I looked at the seat and saw that it had been scrubbed. Whoever had parked the car the night before had steam-cleaned my seat. It was like nothing had ever happened. I asked the valet if he knew anything about the strange person who had done this and he had no idea.

"Umm, seriously, do you know who worked last night? Because I had diarrhea in this seat and now it's all gone."

He gave me a smile that read, "I hate all the guests here." I guess he took it as a joke, and in many ways, it was.

Anyway, it was a true "first-class" miracle. I handed the valet a five-dollar tip (I'm not a millionaire, and he didn't clean it) and drove away. If you're out there, man who cleaned my rental car, thank you.

CHAPTER 22

How I Failed at Differentiating My Two Characters of Bob and Archer

I did the same voice. The end.

My Failure Is an Option

I magine the feeling of accomplishment after training so long and running and finishing a full marathon. You'd remember that moment forever and feel proud that you were able to do what you set out to do. But what if you did the same extensive training, began the marathon, got separated from the pack, got disoriented, turned around, and ran the wrong way for miles, only to find yourself back at the starting line? That's a way better story than finishing a marathon. Not to mention, you probably ran like thirteen miles in that story. That's a lot.

When I die, I will probably be remembered as something of a success. My obituary will list my accomplishments, the family I left behind, and most likely string together some kind words about my career. Nothing about my shortcomings. Only I am privy to the map that outlines my life the way I drew it. A cartographic collage with rivers of misgivings and shame, oceans of mismanaged emotions and finances, archipelagos of overeating, and mountains of self-doubt and petty grievances.

It won't speak eloquently of my penis envy. I have often stated that what I lack in penis size, I make up for in penis envy.

It won't share with the world my unhealthy habit of being perpetually boorish and intellectually unsound. It will specifically omit my predilection for smelling my own feces on toilet paper after I wipe. It will also fail to mention my very frequent and unyielding insistence on being boring while drunk. It won't even hint at that time I drunkenly ordered what I thought was a prostitute on a website only to find out she was a licensed masseuse. All that scented oil wasted on miscommunication.

And it certainly won't reveal that after registering to vote for the first time in 1984, I voted for the Republican Ray Shamie for Senate over John Kerry, just because I liked his slogan: "You can call me Ray!"

But isn't this a fate that most of us share? So much of my life has been a succession of small personal failures, and still, I will be remembered for the good fortune. Isn't the life squandered the real story of mankind, once you take away the will to survive? Walt Whitman wrote,

> *I celebrate myself, and sing myself,*
> *And what I assume you shall assume,*
> *For every atom belonging to me as good belongs to you.*

I loafe and invite my soul,
I lean and loafe at my ease observing a spear of summer
grass.

I lean and loaf. All the time. And yet we don't celebrate the loafing and the leaning. This is the spirit in which I told you my tales. The scope of my indifference fills the air with the fetid stench of the failed spirits who came before me. Look at Whitman's words in this light. In the disquieting light of the freedom to fail.

During the Jewish holiday of Yom Kippur, people of my faith fast for twenty-four hours, and on the night of the fast, they go to synagogue and pray to God to be absolved for the sins they committed that calendar year. Everyone stands and repeats the litany of sins that we ask God to forgive. The list is *endless.* So many sins. And every year, we beseech God to hear our plaintive cries for mercy because, in our hearts, we are all failing all the time, in so many ways. Here's a couple of highlights:

- For the sin which we have committed by frivolity.
- For the sin which we have committed by obduracy.
- For the sin which we have committed in passing judgment.
- For the sin which we have committed by causeless hatred.

- For the sin which we have committed by running to do evil.
- For the sin which we have committed by hardheartedness.
- For the sin which we have committed by a gathering of lewdness.
- For the sin which we have committed by foolish talk.
- For the sin which we have committed by a haughty demeanor.
- For the sin which we have committed by casting off the yoke [of Heaven].
- For the sin which we have committed by a confused heart.
- For the sin for which we incur the penalty of forty lashes.
- For the sins for which we are obligated to bring a burnt offering.

And so many more. So what are we to make of all this? I can tell you that I have reached one very obvious conclusion. Every sin listed, each and every one, would make an excellent band name. C'mon, tell me Casting Off the Yoke is not a really good band name. And Forty Lashes? Fucking gold. And don't tell me some prog-rock kid wouldn't want his first band to be called Obduracy. All kids who are starting a band, check out the full list in the Jewish High Holiday prayer book.

In the end, and I hate to get all preachy, but failure is an option in a verifiable way. So many out there place an undue burden on themselves to succeed at something, whatever it might be, and then if they fail, grow seeds of resentment and hate toward that failure and, as a result, themselves, and in many cases, project that resentment and hatred onto others. The key to failure being an option is a way forward. Failing at something is a signal, but it's not a signifier. It doesn't mean the end of something. Often, it's a springboard toward something better, or worse, but isolating a failure and fueling it with too much pressure to reverse it is never a good path. With this, I will say, I hope you fail well.

THE END

Oh shit, I realize I wanted to give you a more helpful means to fail and provide you the practical guidance you need. How can a book about my failures help you withstand your failures? What did we all learn, beyond "beware of those compelled to succeed"? How in the world does this end again? I guess it must end with my imparting to you a crucial lesson, a lesson that could forever alter the course of your life, a lesson that is simple enough to absorb and one that, if you are suffering, can pull you from doldrums and lead you to a softer place. A lesson that, as told, could prepare you to never fail again. A lesson, that, simply put, could have been written far earlier in this book, so to save you all this trouble . . . but nah, forget it.

THE END 2

About the Author

H. Jon Benjamin is an actor, voice actor, and stand-up comedian. He lives in New York.